Should I Stay or Should I Go?

Deciding Your Future After Betrayal

Dr. Chris Samuels

Should I Stay or Should I Go? Deciding Your Future After Betrayal

Published in the United States

ISBN Paperback:

The names, characters, and stories presented in this book are used fictitiously. Any resemblance to actual people, living or deceased, or real-life events is purely coincidental. The examples and scenarios are intended solely for illustrative and educational purposes.

Dedication

This book is dedicated in gratitude to the partners who came to me at the worst moment of their lives, asking a question no one should have to ask. In choosing to face that question rather than run from it, you showed me what courage truly looks like. Thirty years of witnessing that courage taught me everything these pages contain.

About the Author

I'm Dr. Chris Samuels, a licensed clinical psychologist and Certified Sexual and Relational Therapist (CSRTT) with more than 30 years specializing in sexual addiction treatment and in helping partners heal from betrayal trauma. My work has focused on guiding individuals and couples as they navigate the profound challenges that emerge when sexual addiction is discovered, with the understanding that both partners need support and compassionate care during this critical time. I was among the first clinicians to recognize that sexual addiction typically has its roots in childhood trauma and attachment wounds, and that effective treatment must address these underlying issues rather than focusing solely on behavioral change. This perspective, now increasingly recognized in the field, has shaped my clinical approach and my training of other professionals.

Throughout my career, I have been committed not only to treating individuals and couples but also to expanding the field's capacity to serve those affected by sexual addiction. Through the Sexual Addiction Treatment and Training Institute (SATTI), which I founded in 1992 and continue to direct, I have trained hundreds of clinicians in trauma-based approaches to sexual addiction and betrayal trauma. I am currently completing two additional books that will build on this work, furthering my mission to bring clarity, validation, and effective treatment approaches to everyone impacted by sexual addiction.

Contents

Appendices

You're Not Alone in This

If you're reading this, you're likely in one of the most difficult places you've ever been.

Perhaps you've recently discovered something that shattered your understanding of your relationship and your partner. Maybe you've been living with suspicions, partial truths, or a growing sense that something isn't right. Or possibly you're months into a recovery process and facing the question that brought you to this book: Should I stay or should I go?

Whatever brought you here, I want you to know: you're not alone.

I've worked with partners of sex and porn addicts for over thirty years, and I've sat with hundreds of women in the place where you are now. Each story is unique, but certain threads run through all of them: the shock, the betrayal, the desperate need to understand what happened, the agonizing uncertainty about what to do next.

I've seen the courage it takes to face this situation honestly. I've witnessed the strength that emerges when women stop trying to manage an impossible situation alone and start asking for help. And I've walked alongside partners as they've found their way to decisions they could trust: some choosing to stay and rebuild, others choosing to leave and start fresh. Both paths can lead to healing. Both require tremendous courage.

This book exists to support your journey toward a decision that's right for you. There's no predetermined outcome here, no pressure to stay or leave, forgive or not forgive. Just guidance and companionship as you find your way forward.

Take a breath. You've found help.

What You Might Be Feeling

Right now, you might be experiencing things that feel overwhelming or even frightening. Let me name some of what partners commonly describe, so you know you're not alone–and not losing your mind.

You might feel like you're living in a nightmare you can't wake up from. The life you thought you had has been revealed as partly fiction, and your brain keeps trying to reconcile what you believed with what you now know. This cognitive dissonance is exhausting and disorienting.

You might swing between intense emotions and strange numbness. One moment you're consumed by rage; the next, you feel nothing at all. Sometimes the pain is so acute you can barely breathe; other times you go through the motions of daily life feeling oddly disconnected from everything.

You might feel ashamed, even though you did nothing wrong. Many partners describe feeling humiliated, as if the betrayal reflects something deficient in them. This shame often keeps partners from reaching out for support, which only deepens their isolation.

You might feel crazy. After being lied to, perhaps for years, your ability to trust your own perceptions has been damaged. You might find yourself questioning everything: your memories, your judgment, your sanity.

You might feel terrified about the future. Whether you're contemplating staying or leaving, the path ahead seems impossibly uncertain. How can you make such a monumental decision when you can barely think straight?

All of this is normal. Every bit of it. You're not weak, you're not overreacting, and you're not crazy. You're a human being responding to genuine trauma.

Rebecca's Story

When Rebecca first came to see me, she hadn't slept properly in three weeks. She'd discovered her husband's secret email account by accident (she was trying to find a receipt for a return) and what she found there shattered her world.

"The worst part," she told me, "is that I feel like an idiot. How did I not know? We've been married for sixteen years. I thought we were happy. I thought I knew him."

Rebecca spent our early sessions cycling between rage and grief. She couldn't eat. She'd find herself crying in parking lots, unable to go into the grocery store. She snapped at her children and then hated herself for it. She kept going over the past, trying to identify all the signs she'd missed, all the times she'd believed his lies.

"Everyone keeps asking me what I'm going to do," she said. "My mother thinks I should leave him immediately. My best friend says I should give him a chance. My sister thinks I should pray about it. And I'm just . . . I don't know. I don't know anything anymore. I don't know who he is. I don't even know who I am."

Rebecca's confusion and pain were completely understandable. She was being asked to make one of the most important decisions of her life while in the grip of acute trauma, while her brain was flooded with stress hormones, while her sense of reality had been profoundly destabilized.

I told her what I'll tell you: **You don't have to decide anything right now.**

The decision about whether to stay or go is important. It deserves your clearest thinking, your deepest reflection. And you can't access those when you're in crisis. First, you need to stabilize. You need to understand what you're facing. You need to gather information and begin to heal from the initial shock.

The decision will still be there when you're ready to make it.

Rebecca eventually did make her decision, but not for many months, and not until she'd moved through the processes this book describes. What mattered wasn't the timeline; it was that when she finally decided, she trusted her choice. She'd done the work to reach clarity.

That's what I want for you.

What This Book Offers

This book will walk alongside you as you navigate one of life's most difficult decisions. It won't tell you what to do; that's not something anyone else can decide for you. But it will offer you:

A framework for clarity. At the heart of this book are Five Essential Questions that can help you move from confusion toward understanding what you actually need and want. These aren't exam questions with right and wrong answers. They're companions for your reflection as you gather the information you need to make a decision you can trust.

Understanding of the recovery process. If you and your partner choose to attempt recovery together, you'll encounter important milestones: Disclosure, Impact Letters, Empathy Responses, Transparency Agreements. This book will help you understand what each of these is for, what you're entitled to receive from your partner, and what genuine effort looks like.

Guidance that helps both of you. Here's something important: your partner may genuinely want to do right by you but have no idea how. Most addicts have never learned to be truly honest, to sit with someone else's pain, or to offer genuine empathy. This book includes examples and guidance that can help him understand what you need, not because you're responsible for his recovery but because you deserve his best effort. And sometimes people need help knowing what that looks like.

Permission to trust yourself. After experiencing betrayal and deception, you may doubt your own perceptions and judgment. This book will help you reconnect with your inner wisdom and make decisions based on what you actually observe and experience, not on promises or pressure.

Companionship for the emotional journey. Beyond the practical guidance, this book honors the emotional reality of what you're going through. The fear, the anger, the grief, the moments of hope and despair. All of it deserves acknowledgment and care.

How to Use This Book

You don't have to read this book straight through or master every concept. It's organized to follow the natural progression of recovery work, but you can engage with it however it serves you best.

Some days you might read a full chapter. Other days you might just need to revisit a single paragraph that speaks to where you are. Some sections will feel immediately relevant; others you can return to when you're ready.

If you've just discovered the addiction: Start with the first few chapters to understand what you're facing and how to protect yourself. Don't worry about what comes later. You'll get there when you get there.

If you're in the middle of recovery work: Skip to whatever chapter addresses where you are: Disclosure, Impact Letters, or wherever you find yourself. But consider reading about the Five Questions so you have a sense of what you're ultimately trying to clarify and decide.

If you're at a decision point: The Five Questions chapter and the "Making Your Decision" chapter will be most helpful. But trust your own sense of what you need.

There's no exam at the end. There's no right way to use this book. Take what helps. Leave what doesn't. Come back when you need to. Use the resources in the Appendices, or not.

A Word About Your Partner

Throughout this book, you'll find detailed guidance about what your partner should be doing: how to prepare for Disclosure, what an Empathy Response should include, how to engage with transparency and accountability.

This information is here because **you deserve his genuine, full effort,** and he may not know how to give it without this help.

Most sex addicts have spent years, sometimes decades, avoiding honesty, numbing their emotions, and hiding from intimacy. When they enter recovery, they often genuinely want to do right by their partners but have no roadmap for how. Sexual behavior has been a primary coping mechanism, often from early on. They've never learned to be completely honest. They've never practiced sitting with someone else's pain without defending themselves. They don't know what genuine empathy looks like because they've been disconnected from their own emotions for so long.

The examples in this book aren't standards he must meet perfectly. They're illustrations of what's possible when recovery is genuine: what you're entitled to hope for, what you deserve to receive. They're also guidance for him, showing him what you need so he can work toward offering it.

The sections marked **Pages to Share with Your Partner** are specifically written for him: explanations of what you need and guidance on how he might provide it. You can share these sections with him if that feels helpful, or you can keep this book as your private resource. The choice is yours.

You're not his recovery coach or his therapist. But you can communicate what you need, and this book can help you do that clearly.

And as you witness his efforts—however imperfect—you'll gradually get a sense of whether genuine change is possible. That's what this book is really helping you to assess.

A Word About Language

Throughout this book, I use "he" and "him" to refer to the addicted partner, and "she" and "her" for the partner facing the decision. This reflects the majority of the partners I work with, but I know that addiction affects relationships of all configurations. If you're a man whose female partner struggles with sex addiction, or if you're in a same-sex relationship, please translate the language as needed. The principles remain the same.

I also use the term "sex addiction" throughout, while acknowledging that some professionals prefer other terms like "compulsive sexual behavior," "problematic sexual behavior," or "hypersexual disorder." Whatever language you use, this book is for partners whose significant others have engaged in patterns of sexual behavior, whether that's compulsive pornography use, affairs, visits to sex workers, anonymous encounters, or other behaviors that involved deception, caused harm, and appear to be compulsive in nature.

The Journey Ahead

The path ahead isn't easy. There will be painful moments, confusing days, and times when clarity feels impossible. You may cycle through anger, grief, hope, and despair, sometimes all in the same hour.

That's normal. That's how this works.

But there's also the possibility of genuine clarity. Many partners who've walked this road describe eventually reaching a place where they knew—in their gut, in their bones—what was right for them. Whether that meant staying and rebuilding or leaving and starting afresh, they found their way to a decision they could trust.

That's what I want for you. Not a perfect answer, but a clear one. Not certainty about the future, but confidence in your choice.

You deserve to make this decision from a place of genuine understanding: of yourself, of your partner, of what's actually possible.

This book is here to help you get there.

Take your time. Be gentle with yourself. And remember: you don't have to figure it all out today.

I'm with you on this journey. Let's begin.

1. Discovery

When Everything Changes

The moment of discovery arrives like a thunderbolt, shattering what you thought you knew about your relationship, your partner, and your life together. Whether it came suddenly or gradually, you now find yourself in territory you never expected to navigate.

For some partners, discovery is a single, devastating moment. For others, it's a slow dawning: pieces of a puzzle that finally, horribly, click into place. However it happened for you, everything changed.

The Many Faces of Discovery

Discovery takes many forms:

You might have found explicit messages on his phone while

looking for something innocent. Or stumbled across a dating app he forgot to hide. Or discovered a second phone, tucked away where it wasn't supposed to be.

You might have noticed credit card charges that didn't make sense: hotels in your own city, gifts you never received, subscriptions to sites you didn't recognize. Or found a secret email account. Or realized money was disappearing from your accounts with no explanation.

You might have received a phone call: from his workplace about inappropriate behavior, from a health clinic about test results, from a stranger who thought you should know.

Someone might have told you. A friend who saw something. A family member who couldn't keep the secret anymore. A coworker who felt you deserved the truth.

You might have walked in on something. Found images on his computer. Discovered evidence your child found and should never have seen.

Or he might have told you himself, breaking down and confessing, unable to carry the weight of his secrets any longer. Perhaps he was caught, or nearly caught, and the fear of exposure finally outweighed the fear of honesty.

However discovery happened, the ground shifted beneath your feet. And nothing has been the same since.

Maria's Discovery

Maria had been married for twenty-two years when she found

out. Her husband, Tom, had always traveled for work, and she'd never thought much about it. They had a good marriage, she believed. Three kids, a nice home, regular date nights when he was in town.

The discovery came through their daughter. Seventeen-year-old Emma was using Tom's laptop to print a school paper when a notification popped up, a message from a woman Emma had never heard of, with language that left no room for innocent interpretation.

Emma showed her mother. And Maria's world collapsed.

"The first few hours are a blur," Maria told me later. "I remember sitting on the kitchen floor. I remember Emma crying and apologizing, like it was her fault. I remember Tom coming home and the look on his face when he realized we knew. I remember screaming. I remember silence. I don't remember eating or sleeping for days."

What followed was worse, in some ways. As Tom confessed, in pieces, over weeks, Maria learned that the affairs had been happening for over a decade. Multiple women. Escorts. Apps. A whole secret life running parallel to the one she thought they shared.

"I kept thinking about our anniversary trip to Paris," she said. "How happy I was. And now I don't know. Was he texting someone else while we walked along the Seine? Was he thinking about her when he held my hand? I don't know what was real anymore. I don't know if anything was real."

Maria's experience of discovery—the shock, the physical symptoms, the desperate search through memory trying to separate truth from lies—is shared by almost every partner I've worked with. The details differ, but the devastation is the same.

What You Might Be Experiencing

In the days and weeks after discovery, you may experience things that feel overwhelming and frightening. Understanding that these responses are normal (expected, even) can help you feel less alone and less like you're losing your mind.

Your body may be in crisis.

Trauma doesn't just live in your mind; it lives in your body. After discovery, you might experience:

Physical symptoms that won't let up. Insomnia or sleeping too much. Nausea, loss of appetite, or compulsive eating. Headaches. Muscle tension, especially in your neck and shoulders. Heart palpitations. Shakiness. A feeling of heaviness, like moving through water.

Nervous system dysregulation. Your body's alarm system has been triggered, and it may have trouble turning off. You might startle easily, feel constantly on edge, or experience waves of panic that seem to come from nowhere.

Exhaustion that goes beyond tiredness. The kind of bone-deep fatigue that comes from your system working overtime to process something incomprehensible.

These physical responses aren't weakness. They're your body doing what bodies do when faced with genuine threat. Betrayal is a threat to your sense of safety, your identity, your entire understanding of your life. Your body is responding accordingly.

Your mind may be working overtime.

Obsessive thoughts. Your brain keeps returning to the betrayal, cycling through questions, images, scenarios. You might find yourself mentally reviewing your entire relationship history, looking for signs you missed.

Intrusive images. Unwanted mental pictures of your partner with someone else. These can be especially tormenting and hard to control.

Difficulty concentrating. You might find yourself reading the same paragraph over and over, or forgetting what you were doing mid-task. Your cognitive resources are consumed by processing trauma.

Memory problems. Forgetting appointments, losing track of conversations, blanking on words. This is common during acute stress and usually improves as you stabilize.

This mental churning isn't you being obsessive or unable to "let it go." It's your mind trying desperately to make sense of something that doesn't make sense. Your brain is working to integrate information that contradicts everything you believed.

Your emotions may be intense and unpredictable.

Waves of feeling. Rage, grief, fear, disgust, shame, despair, sometimes cycling through all of them in a single hour. The intensity can be frightening.

Numbness. Sometimes, when emotions are too overwhelming, your system shuts down. You might feel strangely detached, watching your life from outside yourself.

Contradictory feelings. You might love him and hate him in the same moment. Want to fix things and want to burn it all down. These contradictions are normal. They reflect the complexity of what you're facing.

Grief for what you've lost. Even if you ultimately decide to stay, you're grieving: the innocent trust, the relationship you thought you had, the partner you believed him to be, the future that will now be different. This grief is real and deserves acknowledgment.

Your sense of self may feel destabilized.

Questioning your judgment. "How did I not know? What's wrong with me that I didn't see this?" Many partners turn the betrayal into evidence of their own failure.

Feeling foolish. Especially if others knew, or if you defended him against suspicions. The humiliation can be as painful as the betrayal itself.

Loss of identity. If your sense of who you are was tied to your relationship (wife, partner, the one he loved) you might feel unmoored. Who are you now?

Shattered assumptions. You may have believed certain things about the world: that people who love each other don't betray each other, that you could tell if someone was lying, that your partner was fundamentally honest. Those assumptions have been shattered.

This Is Trauma

What you're experiencing has a name: betrayal trauma.

For a long time, the trauma of discovering a partner's sexual betrayal wasn't well understood. Partners were often told they were overreacting, being dramatic, or just needed to "get over it." Some were blamed for their partner's behavior, diagnosed as having somehow enabled it or even told they must have been inadequate, which drove him to seek satisfaction elsewhere.

This is wrong, and it's harmful.

Research now clearly shows that discovering a partner's sexual betrayal creates genuine trauma responses, the same kinds of responses seen in other traumatic experiences. The symptoms you're experiencing aren't character flaws or overreactions. They're evidence that something genuinely traumatic has happened to you.

Understanding this matters because it shapes how you treat yourself. **You're not weak. You're not crazy. You're not making a big deal out of nothing.** You're a person who has experienced a serious emotional injury, and you're responding the way humans respond to such injuries.

This means you need care, support, and time to heal, not pressure to "get over it" and make quick decisions.

The Desperate Need to Know

After discovery, many partners experience an almost overwhelming urge to know everything. You might find yourself:

Searching for more information. Going through his phone, email, computer, financial records. Looking for every piece of evidence you can find.

Asking endless questions. Wanting to know every detail: who, what, when, where, how many times, what did they do, what did he say to her.

Researching online. Googling the other person, looking for images, trying to understand what she had that you don't.

This drive to know can feel compulsive, but it makes sense. You've been living in a false reality, and you desperately need to reconstruct what's true. Your brain can't rest until it has enough information to create a coherent picture.

At the same time, the more you learn, the more painful it becomes. Each new piece of information brings fresh hurt. You might feel caught in a terrible bind: needing to know, but devastated by what you find.

A word of caution: There's a difference between gathering the information you need to understand what you're dealing with and engaging in endless detective work that keeps you trapped in pain. Early on, some investigation may be necessary and appropriate.

But at some point, the formal Disclosure process (which we'll discuss later) is a healthier way to get the complete truth. If you find yourself unable to stop searching, that's a sign you need additional support.

The Pressure to Decide

Almost immediately after discovery, you may feel pressure to make decisions: from him, from family, from friends, from yourself.

He might want to know if you're staying or going. He might be pressing for forgiveness, begging for another chance, or alternatively, might be withdrawn and defensive, leaving you feeling even more alone.

Family and friends might have strong opinions. "Leave him immediately." "Give him a chance." "Think of the children." "Once a cheater, always a cheater." "You made a vow." Everyone seems to know what you should do.

Your own mind might be demanding resolution. The uncertainty feels unbearable. You want to know what's going to happen, what your life will look like, whether this nightmare will end.

Here's what I want you to hear: You don't have to decide anything right now.

The decision about whether to stay or go is important, one of the most important you'll ever make. It deserves your clearest thinking, your deepest reflection. And you cannot access those things while you're in acute trauma.

Right now, your only job is to stabilize. To take care of yourself. To begin to understand what you're facing.

The decision will still be there when you're ready to make it. And you'll be better equipped to make it if you don't rush.

What Helps Right Now

In these early days, focus on the basics:

Safety first. Are you physically safe? If there's any history of violence or if you fear for your safety, address that immediately. Reach out to domestic violence resources if needed.

Basic self-care. Try to eat something, even if you're not hungry. Try to sleep, even if it's fitful. Drink water. Move your body, even if it's just a short walk.

One trusted person. You need at least one person who knows what's happening and can support you without judgment or agenda. This might be a friend, family member, or therapist.

Limited decision-making. Don't make any major decisions right now. You can decide about the relationship later. You can decide about telling people later. Right now, just focus on getting through each day.

Professional support. If you can access a therapist who specializes in betrayal trauma, this is enormously helpful. Additionally, look into support groups for partners of sex addicts (S-Anon, COSA, or similar).

Understanding What You're Facing

As the initial shock begins to settle—though it never fully lifts—you'll want to understand more about what you're dealing with.

Sex addiction is complex, and understanding it can be helpful for your journey. Not because understanding obligates you to stay or forgive, but because it can help you make sense of what's happened and assess what's possible going forward.

Sex addiction typically has roots in childhood.

It usually develops from early trauma: abuse, neglect, emotional unavailability, exposure to inappropriate sexual content, or profound attachment wounds. The addictive behavior starts as a way to cope with pain, to self-soothe, to escape overwhelming feelings.

This means the addiction isn't about you. It isn't about your attractiveness, your worth as a partner, your adequacy in bed. It's a broken coping mechanism that predates your relationship, often by many years.

This doesn't excuse what he did.

Understanding origins isn't the same as excusing behavior. He made choices that hurt you, regardless of why he made them. Your pain is completely valid, and understanding his history doesn't minimize what you've experienced.

Think of it this way: If someone crashed into your car because they were fleeing childhood abuse, you would understand why they were driving recklessly, but your car would still be damaged, and you'd still deserve compensation. Understanding the "why" doesn't erase the harm or your right to be angry about it.

Recovery from sex addiction isn't just about stopping the behavior.

It requires addressing the underlying wounds, developing new coping mechanisms, learning genuine honesty and intimacy, often for the first time. This is deep work that takes years, not weeks.

As you move forward, you'll be watching to see whether your partner is doing this deeper work or just managing the surface. That's not about grading him on a measuring stick. It's about paying attention to what you observe and what your gut tells you.

Holding Two Truths

One of the hardest things about this journey is learning to hold two truths at once:

Truth one: Your partner's addiction comes from his own pain and history. He didn't choose to become an addict. The person you fell in love with—his "healthy self"—is real, and that person may be genuinely struggling against patterns that feel overwhelming.

Truth two: His actions have devastated you. Whatever his reasons, he betrayed your trust, deceived you, and caused you profound harm. Your anger, grief, and hurt are completely justified.

Both of these are true at the same time. You don't have to choose between them.

I think of it as posing two separate questions:

Can I understand why he did this? Maybe, with time and information, you can come to understand the forces that shaped him and drove his behavior.

Does understanding make it okay? No. Never. Understanding and acceptance are different things.

You can understand that he was acting out of his own brokenness while still being furious that he broke you in the process. You can have compassion for his struggle while insisting that his behavior was unacceptable. These aren't contradictions. They're the complex reality of loving someone who has hurt you deeply.

Lisa's Two Truths

Lisa came to me after discovering her husband's pornography addiction, not just occasional use, but hours every day, often instead of being present with her and their young children.

"I keep going back and forth," she told me. "One minute I think, 'He's sick. He needs help. I should support him.' The next minute I think, 'He chose this over me. Over our kids. He's selfish and disgusting.' I feel like I'm losing my mind, going back and forth like this."

I told Lisa that she wasn't losing her mind. She was holding two truths.

"Both things are real," I said. "He does have a problem that has roots in his own history. AND he engaged in behaviors that hurt you and your family. You don't have to pick one. You can be compassionate about his addiction and furious about his actions at the same time."

Lisa cried. "I thought I had to figure out which one was true," she said. "Like, if he's really an addict, then I can't be angry. Or if I'm angry, then I'm not being understanding enough."

"You get to be both," I told her. "You get to be understanding AND angry. Compassionate AND hurt. Willing to consider staying AND clear that what he did was wrong. The **and** is important."

This both/and thinking is one of the most important skills you'll develop on this journey. It allows you to hold complexity without being torn apart by it.

What Lies Ahead

The rest of this book will walk you through the journey ahead: the recovery processes you may encounter, the questions that will help you find clarity, and the ultimate decision about your future.

Here's a brief overview of where we're going:

Caring for Yourself on This Journey (Chapter 2) offers guidance on self-care, building support, and protecting yourself during this vulnerable time.

Five Questions to Guide Your Way (Chapter 3) introduces the framework that will help you move toward your decision. These questions will become companions for your reflection throughout the process.

Disclosure (Chapter 4) explains this formal process where your partner tells you the full truth. You'll learn what you're entitled to, what genuine Disclosure looks like, and what to pay attention to.

Your Impact Letter (Chapter 5) guides you in speaking your truth about how his behavior has affected you. This is your chance to be fully heard.

The Empathy Response (Chapter 6) describes his opportunity to show that he truly understands and feels the impact of his actions. You'll learn what genuine empathy looks like and why it matters.

The Transparency Agreement (Chapter 7) explains how to structure ongoing honesty and accountability. You'll learn what you need to feel safe.

Living in the Questions (Chapter 8) offers guidance for the period of watching, waiting, and letting clarity emerge.

Making Your Decision (Chapter 9) helps you bring everything together and move toward your choice.

If You Choose to Stay (Chapter 10) offers guidance for the path of rebuilding.

If You Choose to Leave (Chapter 11) offers guidance for moving forward.

When There Are Children (Chapter 12) addresses the specific challenges of navigating this with children involved.

Rebuilding Intimacy (Chapter 13) explores the tender territory of physical and emotional closeness after betrayal.

A Final Word (Chapter 14) offers closing thoughts and encouragement for whatever path you take.

The Appendices following Chapter 14 offer you resources for reflection, journaling, and tools to help you move toward clarity.

A Gentle Reminder

Before you move to the next chapter, let me remind you: **You don't have to rush.**

If you're in the early days after discovery, you might only be able to read a few pages at a time. That's okay. If you need to put this book down and come back to it later, that's okay too.

Healing isn't linear, and neither is this process. You'll move forward, then back, then forward again. Some days will feel clearer; others will feel like you're back at square one.

That's not failure. That's how this works.

Be patient with yourself. You're doing something incredibly hard.

When you're ready, the next chapter offers guidance on caring for yourself during this difficult time. Because before you can make good decisions about your relationship, you need to make sure you're okay.

2. Caring for Yourself on This Journey

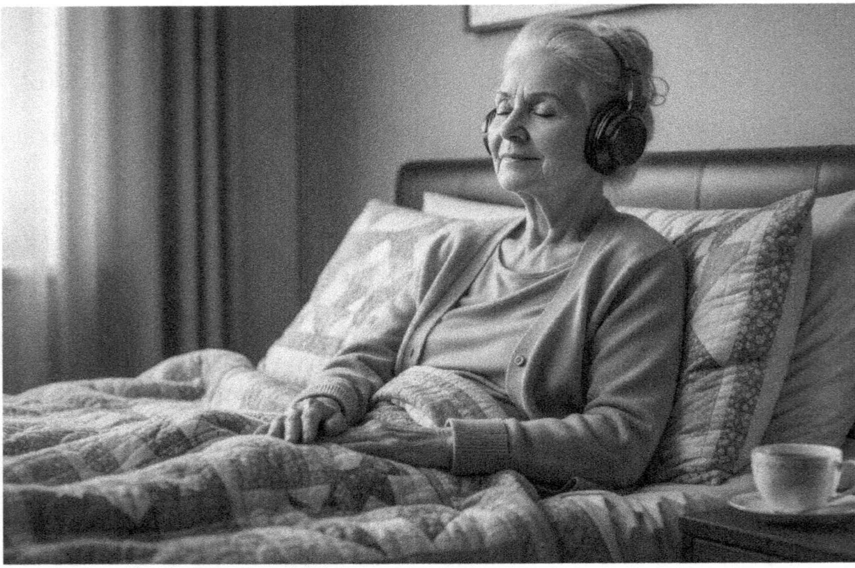

You Matter Too

Before we go any further into the recovery process, the questions that will guide your decision, or what you might expect from your partner, I want to spend time on something essential: You.

In the chaos that follows discovery, it's easy to lose yourself. Your attention gets consumed by his behavior, his recovery, his feelings, what he's doing or not doing. You might be spending hours researching sex addiction, monitoring his activities, trying to figure out what went wrong. Meanwhile, your own needs—physical, emotional, spiritual—can slip into the background.

This chapter is a gentle reminder: **Your well-being matters. Not as an afterthought, but as a priority.**

You cannot make clear decisions from a place of depletion. You cannot accurately assess your relationship if you're running on empty. And regardless of what happens with your partnership, you deserve to be cared for, including by yourself.

The Oxygen Mask Principle

You've heard the instruction on airplanes: In case of emergency, put on your own oxygen mask before helping others.

This isn't selfish. It's practical. If you pass out from lack of oxygen, you can't help anyone, including yourself.

The same principle applies here. You're in an emergency of sorts, an emotional and relational emergency. And while it might feel like all your energy should go toward figuring out the situation, managing his recovery, or holding your family together, the truth is: ***If you don't take care of yourself, you won't have the resources to handle any of it.***

Self-care isn't a luxury right now. It's survival.

Janet's Story

Janet was a doer. A fixer. The one everyone counted on to hold things together.

When she discovered her husband's affairs, her first instinct was to manage the crisis. She researched treatment programs, found him a therapist, located a support group, read every article she she could find on sex addiction. She monitored his phone, checked his location, kept mental notes of his schedule. She managed his recovery like a project.

Meanwhile, she wasn't sleeping. She'd lost fifteen pounds. Not on purpose, but because she couldn't eat. She'd stopped talking to her friends because she was ashamed. She went through the motions at work but couldn't concentrate. She snapped at her kids, then felt guilty. She cried in the shower so no one would hear.

When Janet came to see me, she was exhausted and confused. "I'm doing everything I can," she said. "Why isn't it working? Why do I feel worse instead of better?"

"Janet," I asked gently, "what are you doing to take care of yourself?"

She looked at me blankly. The question didn't compute.

"I don't have time for that," she said. "I have to focus on fixing this."

But Janet couldn't fix anything, not her husband's addiction, not her marriage, not her own pain, while she was running on fumes. Her depletion was affecting her judgment, her emotional regulation, her ability to see clearly. She was trying to make life-altering decisions while in a state of physical and emotional crisis.

Janet's first assignment wasn't about her marriage. It was about sleep. And food. And one conversation with a trusted friend. We had to get her stabilized before we could do anything else.

What Self-Care Actually Means

Self-care has become a buzzword, often associated with spa days and scented candles. But real self-care, especially during crisis, is more fundamental than that.

Self-care means tending to your basic human needs, even when—especially when—you don't feel like it.

Sleep. Your body and brain need rest to process what's happening. Trauma disrupts sleep, so this may be difficult. But prioritizing sleep, maintaining a regular bedtime, limiting screens before bed, considering talking to your doctor if insomnia persists, is essential.

You might not sleep well. That's okay. But creating the conditions for rest matters. Lying in bed ruminating doesn't count; that's suffering, not resting. If you can't sleep, try guided meditations, gentle music, or simply getting up and doing something calming until you feel tired.

Nourishment. You might not feel hungry. Food might seem unappetizing or even nauseating. But your body needs fuel, and your brain can't function properly without it.

You don't have to eat elaborate meals. Simple, nourishing food is fine. Soup. Toast. Fruit. Whatever you can manage. If eating feels impossible, try small amounts frequently rather than full meals. Stay hydrated.

Some partners find they go the other direction: eating compulsively to soothe their pain. If that's you, try to bring gentleness rather than judgment. Your body is trying to cope. But notice if food is becoming another way to numb rather than nourish.

Movement. Your body is holding trauma, and movement helps release it. This doesn't mean you need to train for a marathon.

Walking counts. Stretching counts. Dancing in your living room counts.

Movement also helps regulate your nervous system. When you're stuck in fight-or-flight mode, physical activity can help discharge some of that activation and bring you back to a calmer state.

Connection. Isolation is dangerous right now. Shame often drives partners into hiding; you don't want anyone to know, you don't want to explain, you don't want to see the pity or judgment in their eyes.

But humans are wired for connection, and you need support. Even if you can't tell everyone what's happening, you need at least one person who knows and who can be present with you.

Limits on rumination. Your mind wants to go over and over the betrayal, examining it from every angle. Some processing is necessary, but endless rumination keeps you stuck in pain without moving toward healing.

Try to set some limits. Designate specific times to think about the situation, and practice redirecting your thoughts at other times. This is incredibly hard, but it gets easier with practice.

Permission to Feel What You Feel

Self-care also means allowing your emotions to exist without judgment.

You might feel:

Rage. Towering, consuming fury at what he's done to you. The urge to scream, throw things, hurt him the way he's hurt you.

Grief. Deep, keening sorrow for what you've lost: the relationship you thought you had, the partner you believed him to be, the future you imagined together.

Fear. Terror about what comes next. Will you be okay? Will your children be okay? What will people think? How will you survive?

Shame. That horrible sense that this reflects something wrong with you. That you should have known. That you weren't enough.

Disgust. Revulsion at what he did, who he did it with, the thought of him touching you.

Love. Yes, you might still love him. This can be confusing and make you feel weak or foolish. But love doesn't evaporate on command, even when someone has hurt us deeply.

Numbness. Sometimes the feelings are too much, and your system shuts down. You feel nothing at all, just flat, gray emptiness.

Relief. If you'd suspected something for a long time, there might be a strange relief in finally knowing. This doesn't mean you're not devastated. It just means part of you is glad the uncertainty is over.

All of these are normal. You don't have to justify them, fix them, or make them go away. They're not signs of weakness or instability. They're signs that you're human and something terrible has happened.

Let them come. Let them move through you. They won't destroy you, though they might feel like they will.

Elena's Emotions

Elena was raised to be strong. In her family, you didn't complain. You didn't fall apart. You handled things.

After discovering her husband's double life, she tried to handle it. She told herself she would be mature about this, deal with it rationally, not become "hysterical." She pushed down her anger, blinked back her tears, maintained her composure.

Until she couldn't.

One day, alone in her car after dropping her kids at school, she started screaming. Not crying, screaming! Primal, gut-wrenching screams that came from somewhere deep inside her. She pulled into an empty parking lot and screamed until her throat was raw.

Then she sat there, shaking, terrified. "I thought I was losing my mind," she told me later. "I thought if I let myself feel it, I'd never stop. I'd just dissolve into nothing."

But she didn't dissolve. After the screaming subsided, she felt, not better, exactly, but lighter. Like something had been released.

"I think my body needed that," she said.

It did. Elena's body had been holding that scream for weeks.

When she finally let it out, she wasn't losing control, she was releasing pressure that had built to dangerous levels.

I told Elena what I'll tell you: **Your emotions need somewhere to go.** Keeping them locked inside takes enormous energy and ultimately doesn't work. They'll find a way out eventually: maybe as an explosion of rage, maybe as physical symptoms, maybe as depression.

Better to find safe ways to let them flow: crying, journaling, talking to a trusted person, physical exercise, creative expression. The emotions won't destroy you. Trying to contain them indefinitely just might.

Building Your Support System

You need people around you who can help. Not people who will tell you what to do, but people who can hold space for your pain and walk alongside you during this dark time.

Choosing carefully matters. Not everyone in your life will be able to support you well. Some people:

- Will immediately tell you what you should do, based on their own values or experiences
- Will be so uncomfortable with your pain that they'll try to rush you through it
- Will judge you for staying or for considering leaving
- Will share your situation with others without permission
- Will make it about themselves somehow

- Will minimize what you're going through or suggest you're overreacting

These people, however well-meaning, aren't the ones to lean on right now.

What helpful support looks like:

- Listening without rushing to advice
- Validating your feelings without trying to fix them
- Respecting the complexity of your situation
- Keeping your confidences
- Supporting you whatever you decide
- Checking in without being intrusive
- Letting you lead the conversation
- Being honest but kind

Consider different types of support:

A trusted friend or family member who can know the whole story and be available when you need to talk or just not be alone.

A therapist who specializes in betrayal trauma who can provide professional guidance and a safe space to process. This is different from couples therapy. This is support just for you.

A support group for partners of sex addicts (like S-Anon, COSA, or similar groups) where you can connect with others who truly understand what you're going through.

Your physician if you're experiencing physical symptoms, sleep problems, or need support around anxiety or depression.

You don't have to tell everyone. You get to choose who knows and how much they know. This is your story to share or not share as you see fit. Having a few trusted people is more valuable than broadcasting your situation widely.

A Note on Professional Help

I strongly encourage you to find a therapist if at all possible. Not just any therapist; one who specifically understands betrayal trauma and sex addiction. General therapists, even good ones, sometimes miss the mark with this issue. They might focus too quickly on "your role in the relationship problems" or push you toward forgiveness before you're ready. They might not understand the trauma symptoms you're experiencing.

A specialist will understand:

- That what you're experiencing is genuine trauma
- That your symptoms are normal responses to an abnormal situation
- That you need to heal regardless of what happens with the relationship
- That the timeline for decisions is yours to determine
- That both staying and leaving can be healthy choices depending on circumstances

If cost is a barrier, look into sliding-scale options, therapy training clinics, or online therapy platforms that may be more affordable. 12-Step support groups are free and can be tremendously helpful.

Protecting Yourself

Self-care also means protecting yourself: physically, emotionally, financially, and legally.

Physical safety. If there's any history of violence, intimidation, or if you feel physically unsafe, this is the priority. Reach out to domestic violence resources. Make a safety plan. Don't let anyone minimize your concerns.

Sexual health. If your partner's behavior included contact with others, you need to be tested for sexually transmitted infections. This is awkward and painful, but it's essential. Your doctor can help you determine what tests are appropriate.

Emotional safety. You have the right to set boundaries around conversations and interactions. If talking with your partner leaves you feeling worse (more confused, more destabilized, more hurt), you can limit those conversations. You can say, "I'm not ready to discuss this right now." You can leave the room.

Financial awareness. Make sure you understand your financial situation. Know what accounts exist, what money is available, what debts you have. If you don't already have access to this information, now is the time to get it. This isn't about preparing to leave, it’s about not being in the dark about your own life.

Legal awareness. Depending on your situation, you might want to consult with an attorney, not necessarily to take action, but to understand your rights and options. Knowledge is power, even if you choose not to use it.

Informational boundaries. Be thoughtful about how much time you spend researching, investigating, or monitoring his behavior. Some information-gathering is appropriate, but endless detective work keeps you stuck in pain and hypervigilance. There will be a structured process (Disclosure) for getting the information you need.

Boundaries: What They Are and Why They Matter

Boundaries are limits you set to protect your well-being. They're not about controlling your partner. They're about defining what you will and won't accept, and what you will do if those limits are crossed.

Boundaries are for you, not against him. A boundary isn't a threat or an ultimatum. It's a statement of your own limits and intentions.

The difference:

- **Ultimatum:** "If you ever look at porn again, I'll divorce you." (Focused on controlling his behavior)
- **Boundary:** "I'm not willing to be in a relationship where pornography is present. If I discover it's happening, I'll need to reassess whether I can stay." (Focused on what you're choosing to accept)

Boundaries require follow-through. A boundary you don't enforce isn't really a boundary: it's a wish. Before setting a boundary, ask yourself if you're prepared to follow through on the consequences. If not, it may not be the right boundary to set right now.

Boundaries can evolve. What you need early in this process might be different from what you need later. You can adjust your boundaries as circumstances change.

Some boundaries to consider:

Around communication:

- "I need 24 hours to think before discussing major issues."
- "I won't engage in conversations when either of us is yelling."
- "I need you to answer my questions honestly, even when it's hard."

Around space:

- "I need time alone in the evenings to process."
- "I'm not ready to share a bed right now."
- "I need you to stay elsewhere for a few days while I figure out what I need."

Around his recovery:

- "I need to see you actively engaged in therapy and meetings."
- "I need transparency about where you are and what you're doing."
- "I need you to tell me about any slips or relapses within 24 hours."

Around your own needs:

- "I need to attend my own therapy without you asking what we discussed."
- "I need time with my friends without having to explain myself."
- "I need you to manage your own emotions rather than expecting me to comfort you about this."

When You Don't Feel Like Caring for Yourself

Here's the truth: There will be days when self-care feels impossible. When getting out of bed is a monumental effort. When eating feels pointless. When the pain is so heavy that taking a shower seems absurd.

On those days, be very gentle with yourself.

Minimum viable self-care might mean:

- Drinking a glass of water
- Taking your medications if you have them

- Opening a window for fresh air
- Sending one text to someone who cares about you
- Taking ten deep breaths
- Getting through the next hour

That's it. That's enough for that day.

This won't last forever, even though it might feel like it will. The acute phase of crisis does ease. You will feel more functional again. But right now, if you're in the depths, just surviving is an accomplishment.

Grace's Minimum Days

Grace called them her "minimum days."

"Some mornings I'd wake up and know immediately: this is a minimum day," she told me. "Getting through work wasn't going to happen. Making dinner for my kids wasn't going to happen. Being a functional adult wasn't going to happen."

On minimum days, Grace's only goals were:

- Get the kids to school (even if she drove them in pajamas)
- Drink water
- Eat something, even if just crackers
- Take her anxiety medication
- Text her sister that she was alive

Everything else was optional.

"I felt guilty at first," she said. "Like I was failing. But I've learned that getting through trauma isn't about performing. It's about surviving. And on minimum days, surviving was enough."

Grace's minimum days became less frequent over time. But having permission to have them, without shame, without judgment, was part of how she got through.

Please give yourself that same permission. **On the hard days, surviving is enough.**

Taking Care of Your Whole Self

Self-care encompasses more than the physical. You are a whole person—body, mind, heart, and spirit—and all of these need tending.

Caring for your body: Sleep, food, movement, medical attention as needed. The basics we've discussed.

Caring for your mind: Limiting rumination, seeking information that helps (like this book) while avoiding endless doom-scrolling, engaging in activities that give your brain a break: reading, puzzles, games, anything that occupies your attention in a healthy way.

Caring for your heart: Allowing emotions, connecting with supportive people, engaging in activities that bring comfort or small moments of pleasure: music, nature, time with pets or children, anything that reminds you that life still holds sweetness even amidst pain.

Caring for your spirit: Whatever nourishes you at the deepest level. This might be religious practice, meditation, time in nature, creative expression, journaling, or simply sitting in silence. Many partners find their spiritual lives shaken by betrayal. If your faith has been rocked, that's its own grief to process.

Carla's Spiritual Struggle

Carla's faith had always been central to her life. She and her husband had met at church, married in their congregation, raised their children in the faith community that meant everything to her.

When she discovered his affairs, her spiritual world crumbled alongside her marriage.

"I prayed so hard," she said. "I prayed for our marriage. I prayed for him. I prayed for protection. And this whole time, while I was praying, he was . . . " She couldn't finish the sentence.

Carla felt betrayed not just by her husband, but by God. How could this happen? Why didn't God protect her? Was her faith meaningless?

She stopped going to church. She couldn't face the people there, couldn't sit next to her husband in the pew. She stopped praying. The practices that had always comforted her now felt hollow.

"I feel like I've lost everything," she told me. "Not just my marriage, but my faith, my community, my identity. Who am I if I'm not a Christian wife and mother doing everything right?"

Carla's spiritual crisis was as real as her relational one, and it needed tending. We talked about how faith can hold complexity, how doubt and anger are part of many spiritual traditions, how wrestling with God is actually biblical. We talked about finding safe people within her faith community who could hold her pain without judgment.

Over time, Carla found her way back to a spiritual life, different from before, less certain in some ways, but more honest. Her faith became less about performing and more about being real.

If your spiritual life has been affected by this crisis, know that this is normal and that you're not alone. Give yourself permission to struggle, doubt, rage, or withdraw. And when you're ready, seek out spiritual companions who can hold the complexity with you.

You Are Worth Caring For

Let me close this chapter by saying something directly: **You are worth caring for.**

Not because of what you do for others. Not because of your role as wife or mother or employee. Not because you're handling this crisis well or poorly. You are inherently worthy of care, simply because you're a human being.

The betrayal you've experienced might have shaken your sense of worth. You might feel foolish, unlovable, deficient in some way. Those feelings are understandable, but they're not true.

His behavior was about him: his wounds, his addiction, his failures. They were not about your worth.

You deserve kindness. You deserve rest. You deserve support. You deserve pleasure and joy and peace, even in small moments, even amid crisis.

Caring for yourself isn't selfish. It's necessary. And it's a way of affirming your own value at a time when that value might feel under assault.

So please: Eat something nourishing. Get some rest. Call someone who loves you. Move your body. Let yourself cry.

Find small moments of comfort.

Take care of yourself. The journey ahead requires it. And more importantly, you deserve it.

Reflection Questions

These aren't assignments, just invitations to notice where you are:

- What does my body need right now that I've been neglecting?
- Who in my life can be a safe source of support?
- What emotions have I been avoiding or suppressing?
- What small act of self-care could I do today?
- What boundaries might help me feel safer?

When you're ready, the next chapter introduces the Five Essential Questions: the framework that will guide your reflection as you move toward your decision. Take your time. There's no rush.

3. Five Questions to Guide Your Path

A Framework for Finding Clarity

In the swirl of emotions, questions, and pressures that follow discovery, it helps to have something to hold onto, a framework that can guide your thinking without telling you what to think.

That's what this chapter offers: Five Essential Questions that will become companions for your reflection as you move through this journey.

These aren't exam questions with right and wrong answers. They're not a checklist to complete or a test to pass. Think of them more as lenses, ways of focusing your attention on what matters most as you gather information and work toward a decision you can trust.

You won't answer them all at once. In fact, you probably can't answer them fully yet. They're meant to live with you over time, becoming clearer as you move through the recovery process, witness your partner's efforts, and do your own healing work.

Why These Questions?

After working with partners of sex addicts for over thirty years, I've noticed that the women who find their way to clear, trustworthy decisions tend to wrestle with certain core questions, whether they articulate them explicitly or not.

These questions cut through the noise. They help you focus on what actually matters for your decision rather than getting lost in details that feel urgent but aren't ultimately central.

They also honor the complexity of your situation. There's no simple formula that can tell you whether to stay or go. But there are essential things to understand about yourself, your partner, and your relationship that can guide you toward clarity.

The Five Questions are:

1. Is genuine change happening?
2. Can I feel safe here?
3. Can this relationship honor who I am?
4. Is there enough foundation to build on?
5. What does my deepest wisdom tell me?

Let's explore each one.

Question One: Is Genuine Change Happening?

This is perhaps the most fundamental question. You cannot rebuild a relationship with someone who isn't genuinely changing. Surface compliance (attending meetings, saying the right things, avoiding getting caught) isn't the same as real transformation.

But what does genuine change actually look like? How can you tell the difference between someone who is truly recovering and someone who's just managing the crisis until things calm down?

The Difference Between Compliance and Recovery

Compliance looks like going through the motions. Attending therapy because you insisted. Going to meetings but not really engaging. Saying "I'm sorry" while subtly blaming circumstances or you. Stopping the most obvious behaviors while continuing to hide, minimize, or deceive in other ways.

Compliance is about managing consequences. The motivation is external: avoiding divorce, keeping up appearances, getting you to calm down. When the pressure eases, compliance tends to ease too.

Recovery looks like genuine internal transformation. Engaging deeply with therapy because he has realized he needs it. Attending meetings and finding them meaningful. Working with a sponsor. Taking full responsibility without excuses. Becoming more honest overall, not just about the big things but about small things too. Doing the work even when no one is watching.

Recovery is about changing who he is, not just what he does. The motivation becomes internal. He's doing this because he has recognized something broken in himself and genuinely wants to heal. Recovery continues even when the external pressure decreases.

Signs of Genuine Recovery

A note about early recovery: You're not looking for perfection. Recovery is a learning process where your partner gradually discovers alternative ways to cope with stress, loneliness, and painful emotions. Slips can happen, especially early on, and don't necessarily mean he's not working sincerely. What matters is the overall trajectory: is he becoming more honest about slips? Using them as learning opportunities rather than hiding them? Getting back on track more quickly each time? Genuine recovery shows growth over time, not flawless execution from day one.

As you observe your partner over time, here are some things that might indicate genuine change is happening:

He's doing the deeper work. He's not just managing behavior, but healing the underlying wounds from childhood that made him vulnerable to addiction in the first place. This trauma work is what separates genuine recovery from compliance and white-knuckling.

Is he in therapy that explores his history and the emotional needs his addiction was meeting? Is he making connections between his past and his patterns?

Honesty is increasing. For someone who's spent years hiding and deceiving, complete honesty doesn't happen overnight. But in genuine recovery, you'd expect to see a trajectory toward greater honesty. Is he becoming more forthcoming? Is he telling you difficult truths before you discover them yourself? Is he honest about small things, not just big ones?

He can sit with discomfort. Addiction is often about escape: avoiding painful emotions by numbing out with sexual behavior. Recovery requires developing the ability to feel difficult feelings without running from them. Is he becoming more emotionally present? Can he tolerate discomfort without retreating into old patterns or developing new escape hatches?

He takes full responsibility. Not "I did this because of stress" or "I did this because you weren't available." Not "I know it was wrong, but . . ." Just clean ownership: "I did this. I caused this harm." Does he own his behavior without excuses, without subtle blame-shifting?

His empathy is growing. Can he genuinely feel the impact of his behavior on you? Not just acknowledge it intellectually, but actually feel it? Is his concern about your pain, or mainly about his own guilt and consequences? We'll explore this more in the Empathy Response chapter, but growing empathy is a crucial sign of genuine recovery.

He's accountable without being managed. Is he attending meetings, staying in touch with his sponsor, going to therapy, without you having to remind, push, or monitor? Recovery that requires your constant management isn't really his recovery; it's you managing his behavior.

He's developing genuine self-awareness. Does he understand his triggers, his vulnerabilities, the emotional patterns that feed his addiction? Can he articulate what was driving his behavior and what he's doing differently now?

Rachel's Observations

Rachel spent months watching her husband, David, after discovery. She wasn't sure what to look for, but she paid attention.

"At first, I was looking at the wrong things," she told me. "I was focused on whether he was looking at porn, whether he was where he said he'd be. I was being a detective instead of actually seeing him."

I encouraged Rachel to shift her attention, not to stop being vigilant but to notice different things. How did David talk about his therapy sessions? What happened when she got upset? How did he respond when she asked hard questions?

"I started noticing things," she said. "Like, he used to get really defensive when I was angry. He'd try to manage me, calm me down, explain why I was overreacting. Now he just . . . lets me be angry. He doesn't try to fix it or make excuses. He says things like, 'I understand why you feel that way. I did this to us.'"

Rachel also noticed David talking differently about himself. "He used to act like the addiction was something that happened to him, like he was a victim of it. Now he talks about his behaviors. He talks about what was going on emotionally when he acted out. He's connecting it to stuff from his childhood I'd never even heard about."

Most significantly, Rachel noticed that David was doing recovery work when she wasn't watching. "I found his journal once, not snooping, it was just sitting there. He'd been writing every day. Pages and pages about what he was learning, what he was struggling with, what he wanted to be different. He wasn't doing that for me. He was doing it for himself."

None of this meant Rachel had decided to stay. But it gave her real information: not hopes or promises, but actual observations of genuine change happening.

Red Flags

On the other hand, certain patterns suggest that genuine recovery may not be occurring:

Recovery efforts that depend on your monitoring. If he only does recovery work when you're checking up on him, that's compliance, not recovery.

Continued minimizing or blame-shifting. "It wasn't that bad." "Everyone looks at porn." "If you'd been more attentive . . ." Any version of making the addiction smaller than it is or placing responsibility elsewhere.

More focus on your "moving on" than his growth. Pressure for you to forgive, trust, "get over it," or commit to staying, especially when that pressure is greater than his focus on his own transformation.

Defensiveness when you raise concerns. In genuine recovery, he should be able to hear your worries, fears, and observations without getting defensive. If every concern you raise becomes an argument about whether you're being fair, that's a problem.

Pattern of starting strong and fading. Intensive effort right after discovery that gradually dwindles as the crisis recedes. Recovery isn't a sprint; it's a marathon.

New problematic behaviors replacing old ones. Sometimes addicts stop one behavior but transfer the addiction to something else: working compulsively, drinking more, gaming, developing other escape mechanisms. The underlying pattern hasn't changed; it's just wearing a different costume.

Dishonesty about "small" things. If he's still lying about little things (where he was, who he talked to, why he was late) that suggests honesty hasn't become his new default.

What You're Really Asking

At its heart, **Question One** is asking: ***Is his "healthy self" becoming strong enough to reliably manage his "addict self"?***

Every person with addiction has these two aspects. The healthy self is who they really are: the person capable of love, integrity, genuine connection. The addict self is the part driven by compulsion, willing to lie and betray to get what it wants.

In active addiction, the addict self is in charge. In recovery, the healthy self, if nurtured and supported, gradually takes the lead, developing the strength, tools, and resources to manage the addict self's demands.

Your partner will likely never be "cured" in the sense that the addict self completely disappears. But with genuine recovery, the healthy self can become strong enough that sobriety is sustainable and trust can be rebuilt.

You're watching to see if that's happening.

Question Two: Can I Feel Safe Here?

Safety is non-negotiable for any healthy relationship. After betrayal, your sense of safety has been shattered, and this question asks: ***Can it be rebuilt? Can you establish the conditions you need to feel secure?***

The Many Dimensions of Safety

Safety encompasses multiple dimensions:

Physical safety. Are you free from violence, intimidation, or physical threat? If there's any history of physical abuse, this must be addressed before anything else. You cannot heal, make clear decisions, or rebuild anything if you're afraid for your physical well-being.

Sexual safety. Has your health been put at risk? Have you been tested for STDs? Going forward, are there clear agreements about sexual behavior that protect your physical health?

Emotional safety. Can you express your feelings, including anger, grief, fear, without being punished, dismissed, or manipulated? When you're upset, does he respond with presence and accountability, or with defensiveness and blame? Can you be emotionally vulnerable without it being used against you?

Psychological safety. Can you trust your own perceptions? After being gaslit (being told you were imagining things, were crazy or paranoid), you need to know that your reality won't be systematically distorted and undermined. When you express concerns, are they received as valid? Or are you made to feel unstable, oversensitive, or irrational?

Informational safety. Are you getting the truth? Is he being transparent about his activities, whereabouts, and struggles? Are there people in your social circle who knew about his behavior before you did? Do you still sense secrets, half-truths, and hidden compartments in his life?

Financial safety. Is your economic well-being protected? Has the addiction caused financial damage that needs addressing? Do you have access to information about your financial situation? Do you have resources that aren't completely dependent on him?

Boundaries and Safety

Boundaries are essential to creating safety. They're not about controlling or punishing your partner. They're about defining what you need and what you're willing to accept.

A boundary is a statement of your own limits and what you'll do if they are crossed. It's not an ultimatum designed to control his behavior; it's clarity about what you can and can't live with.

For example:

- "I need you to be in active recovery: therapy, meetings, sponsor contact. If that stops, I'll need to reconsider whether this relationship is viable for me."
- "I need transparency about your whereabouts. If I discover you've been lying about where you've been,

that will be a serious breach of the trust we're trying to rebuild."

- "I can't engage in difficult conversations when you're defensive or dismissive. If that happens, I'll end the conversation and we can try again when you're in a different place."

Boundaries require follow-through. A boundary you don't enforce teaches him that your limits aren't real. So before setting a boundary, ask yourself: Am I prepared to follow through on the consequences?

The Transparency Agreement

We'll discuss this more fully in Chapter 7, but part of creating safety involves establishing structured transparency: clear agreements about how openness and accountability will work going forward.

This might include:

- Sharing devices and passwords
- Location sharing
- Regular check-ins about recovery
- Agreements about disclosing slips or struggles
- Clear protocols for what happens if agreements are broken

How your partner responds to the idea of transparency tells you something important. Does he understand why it's necessary and embrace it willingly? Or does he resist, resent it, call it controlling?

A partner in genuine recovery understands that he destroyed trust and that rebuilding it requires more than words. He accepts transparency not as punishment but as a necessary scaffolding while trust is rebuilt.

Megan's Safety Needs

Megan struggled to feel safe after discovering her husband Brian's years of secret hook-ups through dating apps.

"Even after he deleted the apps and gave me his passwords, I couldn't relax," she said. "I was constantly checking his phone, monitoring his location, asking where he was going. I felt like I was going crazy."

What Megan was experiencing was normal. Her nervous system was stuck in threat-detection mode because it had learned that danger was real. The betrayal had proven that she couldn't trust her sense of safety.

We worked on two things: helping Megan develop structured ways to meet her safety needs (rather than constant, anxious monitoring), and helping Brian understand that her need for transparency wasn't about control, it was about trauma.

"The turning point," Megan told me, "was when Brian stopped acting like my need to check on him was a burden. He started offering information before I asked. He'd text me from his meeting, send me a photo of where he was having lunch, let me know when something came up that changed his schedule. He wasn't doing it because I demanded it. He was doing it because he understood I

needed it."

Brian also learned to respond to Megan's anxiety without defensiveness. "Before, when I'd get worried and check his phone, he'd get annoyed. Like I was insulting him. Now he just says, 'I get it. Check whatever you need.' Something about that calm acceptance actually made me need to check less."

Over time, Megan's sense of safety did begin to rebuild. Not quickly. It took well over a year. But the combination of genuine recovery, consistent transparency, and Brian's patient understanding of her trauma gradually calmed her nervous system.

"I still have moments," she said. "But I don't live in constant fear anymore. I actually believe him when he tells me where he's going. That felt impossible a year ago."

What If Safety Can't Be Established?

Sometimes, despite best efforts, safety cannot be established within the relationship. This might be because:

- The partner is not genuinely recovering, so the threat remains active
- The partner resists or undermines transparency and accountability
- The trauma is so severe that the partner's presence continues to trigger overwhelming fear
- There's a pattern of boundary violations that erodes trust faster than it can be rebuilt

- The partner becomes threatening, manipulative, or retaliatory when boundaries are set

If safety cannot be established, that's crucial information for your decision. **You cannot heal, thrive, or build a healthy relationship in an environment where you don't feel safe.** Safety is the foundation everything else depends on.

What You're Really Asking

Question Two is asking: ***Can the conditions I need to feel secure be created and maintained in this relationship?***

This involves assessing both what you need and whether your partner is capable of providing it. Some needs might be met with time and genuine recovery. Others might reveal fundamental incompatibilities.

As you move through the recovery process, pay attention to how you feel. Is your sense of safety growing over time? Are there structures in place that help you feel more secure? Is he contributing to your safety or undermining it?

Your gut will tell you a lot about this question. Even if you can't fully articulate it, you know whether you feel safe or not.

Question Three: Can This Relationship Honor Who I Am?

This question invites you to reconnect with yourself, your values, your needs, your sense of who you are and want to be—and to assess whether this relationship can honor those things.

Reconnecting With Your Core Values

Betrayal often leaves partners feeling disconnected from themselves. In the chaos of discovery and its aftermath, you may have lost touch with what you actually value, need, and want. This question asks you to find your way back.

What matters most to you in a relationship?

Take some time to actually think about this. Not what you think should matter, or what others say should matter, but what genuinely matters to you.

Perhaps it's honesty: knowing you can trust what your partner tells you. Perhaps it's emotional intimacy: feeling truly known and connected. Perhaps it's fidelity, respect, partnership, shared spiritual values, humor, stability, passion. There's no right answer. Only your answer.

What do you need to feel fulfilled? Not just satisfied, but truly thriving?

Again, this is personal. What nourishes you in a relationship? What drains you? What makes you feel alive and valued? What makes you feel diminished?

Caroline's Values Journey

Caroline thought she knew what she valued in her marriage. Security. Family. Commitment. Keeping her vows.

After discovering her husband Mark's multiple affairs, she found herself questioning everything.

"I always said I could never forgive an affair," she told me. "That was my line. But now that it's real, I'm not sure. Does that make me a hypocrite? Does it mean I don't really value fidelity?"

I encouraged Caroline to go deeper. "What does fidelity actually mean to you?" I asked. "Why does it matter?"

As she explored, Caroline realized that fidelity wasn't really about sex for her. It was about being chosen. About being her partner's person. About knowing that when the world got hard, they had each other.

"The sex with someone else hurts," she said. "But what hurts more is the lying. The double life. Feeling like I wasn't enough, or like I was interchangeable. I need to know I matter. I need to know I'm his person."

This clarity helped Caroline think about what she'd need to stay. Not just an end to pursuing affairs, but real evidence that she mattered, that Mark was choosing her, not just defaulting back to her because his latest affair ended.

It also helped her recognize something else. "If I stay and he cheats again, I couldn't survive that. Before, I can maybe understand. He was broken, he was running from something, he made terrible choices. But if it happened again, it would mean I don't matter enough. And that's not something I can live with."

Caroline was clarifying her values, not the abstract ones she'd always claimed but the real ones that would guide her decision.

What the Relationship Requires

Once you're clearer on your values and needs, the harder question emerges: ***Can this relationship, even with genuine recovery, honor them?***

This isn't about what your partner promises. It's about your honest assessment of what's possible.

Some questions to sit with:

Has something been fundamentally broken that can't be repaired? Some betrayals wound so deeply that the relationship can never feel the same, regardless of recovery.

Can you be your authentic self here? Not the performing, managing, hypervigilant self, but your real self? Can you relax, be vulnerable, be imperfect?

Do your values align enough? Now that the illusions have been stripped away, do you and your partner actually want the same things?

Can your essential needs be met? Not every need, but the core ones? The ones that, if unmet, would leave you chronically unfulfilled?

When Values Have Shifted

Sometimes this process reveals that your values have changed. What you thought you could live with before discovery is different from what you know you need now.

This isn't inconsistency; it's growth. Trauma has a way of clarifying what actually matters. The things you thought were negotiable might reveal themselves as essential. The compromises you made might no longer feel acceptable.

Trust this evolution. Your clearer sense of self is valuable, even if it makes the decision harder.

What You're Really Asking

Question Three is asking: ***Can I be fully myself, honored, valued, fulfilled, in this relationship? Or would staying require me to abandon or diminish essential parts of who I am?***

This is deeply personal. Only you can answer it. And the answer might not be clear yet. It might emerge slowly as you heal, as you watch the recovery process unfold, as you reconnect with yourself.

Question Four: Is There Enough Foundation to Build On?

Rebuilding a relationship after betrayal isn't renovation, it's construction from the ground up. This question asks whether there's sufficient foundation for that massive undertaking.

Looking Beneath the Addiction

The addiction and betrayal are real, and they're devastating. But they're not the complete picture of your relationship. Question Four asks you to look at what else exists: what foundation, if any, lies beneath the rubble.

What genuine connection existed before or alongside the addiction?

Was there a friendship at the core of your relationship? Shared values? Mutual respect? Genuine care for each other's well-being? Meaningful history?

When you experienced those good moments, the times he was truly present, caring, emotionally available, you were connecting with his healthy self. That part of him was real. It existed alongside the addict self, operating in separate compartments.

These are raw materials for rebuilding. If they exist, even if they've been damaged, there may be something to work with. Recovery is about strengthening the healthy self so it can be consistently present, not just in glimpses.

But if those genuine connections don't exist, if the relationship was always more about dysfunction than authentic connection, if you rarely or never experienced his healthy self, that's important to acknowledge.

Is there love?

This seems like an obvious question, but it's worth asking directly. Do you love him? Not just familiarity, or fear of being alone, or investment in the life you've built. Actual love.

And equally important: Do you believe he loves you? Not the addicted part of him that was willing to betray you, but his healthy self: does it genuinely love you?

Love alone isn't enough. But its presence or absence matters.

Linda's Foundation

Linda had been married for thirty-one years when she discovered her husband Robert's secret sexual encounters.

"I wanted to hate him," she said. "It would have been easier if I could just hate him. But I couldn't. Underneath my rage, I still saw the man I fell in love with. The man who held my hand when my mother died. The man who made me laugh, who knew me better than anyone."

Linda was wrestling with a genuine foundation. Her relationship with Robert wasn't built only on illusion. There was real love, real partnership, real history.

"But I also had to ask myself," she continued, "whether what we had was strong enough to survive this. Whether we could build something new on top of thirty-one years of lies."

For Linda, the foundation existed. But it was damaged, and she couldn't know if it was strong enough until she and Robert tested it: through the recovery process, through genuine effort, through time.

Other partners I've worked with have reached different conclusions. Some discovered that what they thought was a foundation was actually just familiarity or fear. Some realized the relationship had always been troubled, and the addiction was just the latest chapter. Some found there was genuine love but not enough else to build on.

His Willingness to Build Something New

Foundation isn't just about what exists between you: it’s also about his capacity and willingness to construct something different.

Does he understand that you can't go back to how things were?

The old relationship—the one built partly on deception—is gone. If he's focused on "getting back to normal," that's a problem. There is no normal to go back to.

Is he committed to creating something new?

Recovery isn't just about stopping bad behavior. It's about building a new way of relating, more honest, more intimate, more real. Is he engaged in that project? Does he understand what it requires?

Does he have the patience for the long work?

Rebuilding takes years, not months. There will be setbacks, difficult conversations, moments when giving up seems easier. Is he prepared for that? Does he have the resources, internal and external, to sustain the effort?

The Outside Support

Rebuilding also requires scaffolding: external support that holds things steady while the construction happens.

Therapeutic support. Individual therapy for both of you, and eventually couples therapy with someone who specializes in this area.

Recovery community. His engagement with meetings, sponsors, and accountability partners.

Your support system. Friends, family, support groups: people who can sustain you through the long process.

Time and resources. Emotional bandwidth, practical stability, enough room in your lives to do this work.

If these supports aren't available, rebuilding becomes much harder. Not impossible, but harder.

What You're Really Asking

Question Four is asking: ***Is there enough good here, enough love, respect, history, willingness, to justify the enormous effort of rebuilding? And is that effort actually possible given who he is, who I am, and the support available?***

This isn't about whether rebuilding would be nice. It's about whether it's feasible and worthwhile.

Question Five: What Does My Deepest Wisdom Tell Me?

After all the analysis (watching his recovery, assessing safety, reflecting on values, evaluating foundation), this final question asks you to access a different kind of knowing.

What does your gut tell you? What does your body know? What does your deepest wisdom say?

Beyond Analysis

The first four questions engage your mind, observing, assessing, evaluating. That work is essential. But the final question asks you to access something beyond analytical thinking.

We have ways of knowing that aren't purely rational. Call it intuition, gut feeling, inner voice, embodied wisdom. Whatever language fits for you. It's the part of you that sometimes knows things before you can explain why.

This kind of knowing is especially important when facing complex decisions where the data is mixed, where pros and cons exist on both sides, where there's no obvious right answer.

Learning to Listen

After betrayal, many partners struggle to trust their inner voice. After all, that voice didn't warn them about the addiction. Or worse, it did warn them and they dismissed it. How can you trust something that failed you before?

Here's the thing: Your intuition probably didn't fail you. More likely, you received inner signals that something was wrong, but you overrode them. Because he had explanations, because you wanted to believe him, because admitting the truth was too frightening.

Many partners, looking back, can identify moments when they knew something wasn't right. A feeling in the gut. A hesitation they couldn't explain. A part of them that didn't believe his excuses even as they accepted them.

Your inner wisdom was likely speaking all along. The challenge wasn't hearing it, it was trusting it.

As you heal and gather accurate information through the

recovery process, your intuition becomes more reliable, not less. It has better data to work with. And you're developing the capacity to trust it rather than override it.

Ways of Accessing Deeper Wisdom

Here are some ways to tap into this kind of knowing:

Body awareness. Notice what happens in your body when you contemplate different options. When you imagine staying and rebuilding, what do you feel physically? Tension? Opening? Heaviness? Peace? When you imagine leaving, what do you feel? Our bodies often know before our minds do.

Quiet reflection. Find moments of stillness, away from the noise of other people's opinions, away from the pressure to decide. In that quiet, what arises? What does the still, small voice say?

Imagining your future self. Picture yourself five years from now, having stayed and rebuilt. What do you see? How does that future self feel? Now picture yourself five years from now, having left. What do you see? What does that future self feel? Which vision feels more aligned with who you want to be?

The friend question. If your best friend were in exactly your situation—with everything you know—what would you hope for her? What would you encourage her to do?

Noticing what you already know. Sometimes we pretend not to know things we actually know. If you let yourself be completely honest (no performance, no should's, no fear of consequences), what do you already know about this situation?

Denise's Wisdom

Denise spent months analyzing her situation. Her husband Kevin was doing real recovery work. Safety structures were in place. There was genuine love and history between them. By most measures, rebuilding was possible.

But something kept nagging at her.

"On paper, it makes sense to try," she told me. "He's doing everything right. But when I imagine my future with him, I feel . . . tired. Just tired. Like the road ahead is so long and hard, and I'm not sure I have it in me."

I encouraged Denise to pay attention to that tiredness. Not to make it the final answer, but not to dismiss it either.

Over the next few weeks, she sat with it. She realized the tiredness wasn't just about the work of rebuilding. It was something deeper.

"I think I've been unhappy for a long time," she finally said. "Not just since discovery. For years. The addiction made it worse, but even if there'd been no addiction, I'm not sure this relationship was what I wanted."

Denise's deeper wisdom was telling her something her analytical mind had been avoiding. The addiction was real, and it mattered. But it was also obscuring a more fundamental question about whether this relationship had been right for her all along.

Not every partner will reach Denise's conclusion. Others find that their deeper wisdom says something different; that despite everything, this relationship is worth fighting for. That underneath the pain, there's something real and valuable.

The point isn't what the wisdom says. The point is that it speaks, and it deserves to be heard.

When Wisdom Is Unclear

Sometimes you go inside and there's no clear voice. Just confusion. Fog. Conflicting signals.

That's okay. It might mean you need more time. More information. More healing before the clarity can emerge.

Don't force it. Wisdom tends to arise when conditions are right, when you're calm enough to hear it, when you have enough information to inform it, when you're ready to receive what it has to say.

Keep living the questions. The answer will come.

What You're Really Asking

Question Five is asking: ***Beyond all the analysis, what do I actually know? What is my deepest self telling me about whether to stay or go?***

This isn't about ignoring everything else. It's about integrating it: letting all the information, observations, and reflections settle, and then listening for the truth that emerges.

Living With the Questions

You now have the framework: Five Essential Questions that will guide your journey toward a decision.

But here's what I want you to remember: **You don't need to answer these questions yet.**

They're meant to live with you as you move forward. The recovery processes ahead—Disclosure, Impact Letters, Empathy Responses, Transparency Agreements—will give you opportunities to gather information that helps you answer them.

Question One (Is genuine change happening?) will become clearer as you observe him over time, witness his response to Disclosure, and see how he handles the Empathy Response.

Question Two (Can I feel safe?) will become clearer as you establish boundaries, create transparency structures, and see whether they're honored.

Question Three (Can this relationship honor who I am?) will become clearer as you reconnect with your values through your own healing work and see what the relationship actually offers.

Question Four (Is there enough foundation?) will become clearer as you move through the recovery process together and discover what's real that remains beneath the damage.

Question Five (What does your deepest wisdom say?) will become clearer as you heal, gather information, and create space for your inner voice to speak.

Keeping Notes

It might help to keep a journal as you move through this process. Not obsessive documentation, but periodic notes on what you're observing, feeling, and sensing.

After major events (Disclosure, presenting your Impact Letter, receiving his Empathy Response), take some time to write down your impressions. What did you notice? What did you feel? What does your gut tell you about what you witnessed?

These notes will be valuable later when you're ready to bring everything together and make your decision.

Patience With the Process

Finding your way to a clear decision takes time. Some partners know within weeks; others need a year or more. There's no right timeline, only the timeline that leads you to a decision you can trust.

Give yourself permission to not know yet. The questions will become clearer as you gather more information and do your own healing work.

And when you're ready, when clarity emerges, you'll know. Not with perfect certainty, but with enough confidence to act.

Reflection

You might take some time to sit with each question, not trying to answer definitively, but just noticing where you are right now:

Question One: What have I observed so far about whether genuine change is happening?

Question Two: Do I feel safe? What would I need to feel safer?

Question Three: What are my core values and essential needs? Can I imagine them being honored here?

Question Four: What foundation exists beneath the addiction and betrayal?

Question Five: When I get quiet, what does my deepest self whisper?

You don't need answers. Just notice what arises.

When you're ready, the next chapter explores Disclosure: the formal process where your partner tells you the full truth. This is often one of the most difficult experiences in the recovery process, but also one of the most important. Understanding what you're entitled to and what genuine Disclosure looks like will help you gather the information you need.

Take your time. There's no rush.

4. Disclosure

The Gift of Truth

One of the most painful—and potentially healing—moments in recovery is Disclosure: the moment when your partner finally tells you the full truth about his addiction and behaviors. After months or years of lies, this truth feels both devastating and strangely relieving. You're finally standing on solid ground, even if that ground might also feel like it's shifting beneath you.

But this isn't something that happens immediately. Disclosure is a formal, guided process that requires careful timing and preparation.

The Timing and Process of Disclosure

Disclosure shouldn't happen in the immediate crisis of discovery. Your partner needs to have achieved some stability in his sobriety first, typically at least 90 days, sometimes longer.

Why? Because Disclosure done too early, when he's still in crisis or the addiction is still active, often results in incomplete honesty. He may still be in denial about the extent of his behavior, still minimizing, still unable to face the full truth himself.

Disclosure works best when he's:

- Established consistent sobriety (no acting-out for at least 3 months)
- Been working with a therapist who specializes in sexual addiction
- Completed a thorough inventory of his behaviors
- Developed enough emotional stability and a support system to help him tolerate the conversation
- Prepared with his therapist for what this will require and for its potential aftermath (shame and guilt that might threaten his sobriety)

This is a therapeutic process, ideally facilitated by a trained professional who can guide both of you through it safely.

What Disclosure Will Feel Like

This will be one of the most difficult experiences you'll face on this journey. It's also one of the most important.

I won't sugarcoat it: Disclosure is painful. Hearing the details of your partner's betrayal, laid out completely and honestly, can feel like being wounded all over again. Many partners describe it as one of the hardest days of their lives.

And yet most partners who go through a well-prepared Disclosure say they're ultimately glad they did. Not because it didn't hurt—it did, terribly—but because it gave them something essential: the truth.

Why Disclosure Matters

You've been living with partial truths, suspicions, and the disorienting experience of not knowing what was real. Your mind has probably been working overtime trying to piece together a coherent picture from fragments: lies you've uncovered, his partial admissions, drips of information he's revealed, your own intuitions.

This mental labor is exhausting. And it never quite succeeds, because you're trying to complete a puzzle while someone keeps hiding the pieces.

Disclosure offers you something you deserve: the complete picture. Not so you can be hurt more, but so you can finally stop guessing. So you can know what you're actually dealing with. So you can make decisions about your future based on reality rather than on shifting sands.

Disclosure also reveals something important about your partner. How he approaches this process (how honestly he engages, how thoroughly he prepares, how he handles your pain) shows you something crucial about his capacity for genuine recovery. It's not just what he says; it's how he says it and what it costs him to say it.

A partner who can face the full truth of what he's done, take complete responsibility, and sit with your pain without defending himself, that partner is demonstrating something real. A partner who hedges, minimizes, trickle-truths, or makes the process about his own feelings, that partner is showing you something too.

The Problem with Partial Truth

You might wonder: Do I really need to know everything? Wouldn't it be better to just move forward without all the painful details?

I understand the appeal of this thinking. But experience has taught me that partial truth doesn't work.

Partial truth keeps you in detective mode. When you sense there's more you don't know, you can't stop looking. You check his phone, analyze his stories, watch for inconsistencies. You're constantly on guard because your nervous system knows the full threat hasn't been revealed.

Partial truth makes real intimacy impossible. Intimacy requires knowing and being known. If there are significant secrets between you, genuine closeness can't develop. There's always a wall, even if you can't see it clearly.

Partial truth usually comes out eventually. The things he doesn't tell you in Disclosure have a way of emerging later: through slips, through your detective work, through his guilty conscience. And each new revelation retraumatizes you and destroys whatever trust had started to rebuild.

Partial truth is still a form of control. When he decides what you get to know, he's still managing you, still controlling the narrative, still treating you as someone who can't handle the truth. That's not partnership; it's continued undermining and deception.

Tanya's Experience with Trickle-Truth

Tanya's husband confessed to having an affair. She was devastated, but she appreciated his honesty. They started therapy. He seemed genuinely remorseful. She began to believe they could work through it.

Three months later, she discovered he'd had not one affair but three. Over seven years.

"The first disclosure was bad," she told me. "But the second one, finding out he'd lied even while supposedly coming clean, that was worse. Because now I knew he was capable of looking me in the eye, crying, apologizing, and still holding back the truth."

Tanya and her husband eventually did a proper, therapeutic Disclosure: the full truth this time, with professional guidance. It was awful. The scope of the betrayal was far beyond what she'd been told or imagined.

But something shifted afterward.

"At least I knew," she said. "For the first time since this started, I wasn't wondering what else was out there. The monster was out of the closet. It was huge and ugly, but at least I could see it. I could stop imagining and start dealing with what was actually real."

Tanya's nervous system, which had been on constant high alert, began to settle. Not because the truth was good (it wasn't), but because her body finally knew what it was dealing with.

"The trickle-truth was actually more traumatic than the full disclosure," she reflected. "Because with trickle-truth, I could never trust that I had the whole picture. I was always waiting for the next shoe to drop. After the full disclosure, the shoes had all dropped. I could grieve what was real instead of fearing what might be."

What You're Entitled To

You deserve a Disclosure that is:

Complete. Not the version he thinks you can handle. Not the version that makes him look least bad. The full truth: the types of behaviors, when they occurred, how often, with whom, over what time period, money spent, health risks involved. All of it.

Prepared. A meaningful Disclosure doesn't happen spontaneously. It requires him to work with his therapist beforehand to ensure he's being thorough (not unconsciously "forgetting" things that are particularly shameful), to prepare himself emotionally, and to understand how to be present with your pain. You shouldn't have to drag information out of him or discover later that he left out significant details

Accountable. He should take full responsibility without blaming you, circumstances, stress, or anything else. "I did these things. There's no excuse." Not "I did these things because our relationship was struggling" or "I did these things because I was stressed at work."

Focused on your needs. This is for you, not for his relief. While unburdening himself may bring him some relief, the purpose of Disclosure is to give you the truth you need. He should be focused on your experience throughout, not on his own catharsis or absolution.

Appropriately bounded. There's a difference between complete honesty and gratuitous detail. You need to know what happened, but you don't need graphic descriptions that will create traumatizing mental images. A skilled therapist will help him understand this distinction: comprehensive without being overly explicit.

What Disclosure Might Include

Because most addicts have never done anything like this before, it helps for your partner to understand what comprehensive Disclosure typically covers. The following isn't a rigid checklist, but it gives you a sense of what you're entitled to know:

Types of acting-out behaviors. What did he actually do? Pornography, affairs, hookups, escorts, massage parlors, chat rooms, cam sex, dating, dating apps: whatever forms the addiction took.

Timeline. When did these behaviors start? Were there periods of more or less activity? When did they last occur?

Frequency. How often was this happening? Daily? Weekly? During certain periods?

Other people involved. If there were affairs or encounters with other people, who were they? Were any of them people I know? People in our social circle, workplace, or community?

Money spent. How much money went to the addiction? Did you support some of your acting-out partners? From what sources did you take the money? Are there financial consequences I need to know about?

Health risks. Were there encounters that put my physical health or yours at risk? You need this information to make informed decisions about STD testing and your own safety.

Lies and deception. What specific lies were told to cover the behavior? This can help you understand which memories and experiences were contaminated by deception.

Legal issues. Were there any legal risks or consequences: arrests, workplace incidents, blackmail or threats of exposure?

Privacy concerns. Were there people in our social circle or within our family who were aware of his behavior? Did he tell any of them what he was doing?

"But What If He Didn't Tell Me Everything?"

Such doubts after Disclosure are understandable. It's one of the most common concerns partners have brought to me after the experience.

After all, you've been lied to for months or years. You've discovered that your sense of reality was completely wrong. You've learned he was capable of extraordinary deception while looking you in the eye and swearing his honesty.

So when he finally sits down and tells you the truth, or what he claims is the truth, why should you believe this is different? Why should you trust that now he's being completely honest when he wasn't before?

You're desperate for reassurance: "Is this everything? Can I finally stop bracing for the next terrible discovery? Can I build my healing on solid ground, or will the floor drop out again in six months when I learn there was more?"

This need for certainty is completely legitimate.

But here's an important reality: Perfect completeness isn't always possible. In the fog of compulsive behavior, acting-out in dissociative states, addicts often genuinely don't remember every incident. The brain doesn't form clear memories during periods of intense arousal, shame, and secrecy. What matters isn't achieving a perfect accounting of every act, it’s whether he made a sincere, rigorous effort to be as comprehensive as possible.

Some therapists recommend polygraphs to verify Disclosure completeness. While this can provide reassurance for some couples, what ultimately matters more is what you observe over time: Is he demonstrating genuine transparency in his daily life? Is he voluntarily disclosing uncomfortable truths without being caught? Is he growing in his capacity for emotional honesty and intimacy? These ongoing behaviors are more meaningful than any single test.

Disclosure isn't just about information transfer: it’s about his willingness to be fully known, flaws and all. That willingness, demonstrated consistently over time, is what rebuilds trust.

Helping Him Prepare

Your partner may genuinely want to give you an honest, complete Disclosure but have no idea how. This is where professional guidance matters, and where some of the material in this book can help.

He should be working with his sponsor and a therapist who specializes in sex addiction to prepare his Disclosure. This preparation typically involves:

- Documenting all acting-out behaviors thoroughly (addicts often "forget" things that are particularly shameful; careful documentation helps ensure completeness)
- Preparing emotionally to handle the process without falling apart
- Learning how to take responsibility without excuses or blame-shifting
- Understanding how to be present with your pain and not making it about what he’s feeling
- Practicing appropriate boundaries around graphic detail

You can share this section with him if that feels right. You might say: "This describes what I need from Disclosure. Please read it and work with your therapist to prepare your Disclosure to be able to meet what I am asking for."

Pages to Share With Your Partner: Preparing for Disclosure

The following section is written directly to your partner. You can share it with him if you think it would help him understand what you need.

Your partner has asked you to read this because she needs the following from you: the complete truth about your addiction and acting-out behaviors, delivered in a way that demonstrates genuine accountability and care for her experience.

This is called Disclosure, and it may be one of the most difficult things you ever do. It requires you to face the full reality of your behavior, speak it aloud, and witness the pain it causes the person you love.

It's also one of the most important things you can do both for your recovery and for any possibility of rebuilding your relationship.

Why Disclosure Matters

Your partner has been living in uncertainty, not knowing the full extent of your behavior, not knowing what was real and what was lies, not knowing what else might still be hidden. This uncertainty is its own kind of torture. It keeps her nervous system on constant alert, unable to relax because the full threat remains unknown.

Disclosure ends that uncertainty. It gives her the complete picture so she can finally stop imagining and start dealing with what's actually real. It also demonstrates something crucial about your recovery: that you're capable of complete honesty, that you can take full responsibility, that you can put her needs ahead of your comfort.

How to Prepare

Work with your therapist and sponsor to prepare thoroughly. This typically means:

Document everything. Write down all your acting-out behaviors: types, timeline, frequency, other people involved, money spent, lies told. Be thorough. It's common to unconsciously "forget" things that feel particularly shameful. Push yourself to remember everything, even the things that make you cringe.

Check your completeness. Are there things you're hoping she won't ask about? Things you're telling yourself weren't "that bad" or "don't really count"? Those are the things you most need to include. Incomplete disclosure will do more harm than good.

Prepare emotionally. This process will be painful for you too. Work with your therapist and sponsor on managing your own feelings so you can be present for her rather than collapsing into your own guilt or shame.

Practice taking responsibility. No excuses. No "but." No blaming circumstances, stress, her behavior, or anything else. Practice saying, "I did this. I caused this harm." Clean accountability, nothing else.

Understand the difference between comprehensive and graphic. She needs to know what happened, but she doesn't need graphic sexual descriptions that will create traumatizing mental images. Tell the truth completely but without unnecessary detail that serves no purpose except to wound.

What Your Disclosure Might Sound Like

This isn't a script to recite, but an illustration of the spirit of what's needed:

"Before I begin, I want you to know that I'm committed to being completely honest with you. You deserve the full truth, and I'm going to tell it to you, not because it's easy, but because you've been living with lies for too long and you deserve to know what you're actually dealing with.

"What I'm about to share will be painful. I wish I could spare you that, but I can't undo what I've done. All I can do is finally be honest.

"I'm not going to make excuses or blame anyone else. Everything I'm about to tell you were my behaviors. They are my responsibility.

"[Here you would share the complete truth about your behaviors: what you did, when, with whom, how often, money spent, health risks, lies told to cover it up.]

"I know this is devastating to hear. I know I've caused you unimaginable pain. Your feelings about this, whatever they are, are completely valid. I'm not asking for forgiveness or any particular response. I'm just finally giving you the truth you deserve.

"I'm committed to my recovery, not just to stop the behaviors, but to understand why I did this and to become someone capable of genuine honesty and intimacy. Whether you choose to stay or go, I need to do this work for myself.

"I'm sorry. Not sorry I got caught; sorry for every lie, every betrayal, every moment of pain I've caused you. You didn't deserve any of this."

During Disclosure

When you're actually in the room with her, delivering this truth:

Stay focused on her. This is about giving her what she needs, not about unburdening yourself. Keep your attention on her experience.

Don't defend or explain. When she reacts with pain or anger, don't try to defend yourself or explain why you did things. Just receive her response. "I understand why you feel that way" is appropriate. "But you have to understand that I was under a lot of pressure" is not.

Let her feel what she feels. Don't try to manage her emotions. Don't tell her to calm down. Don't try to fix her pain. Just be present with it.

Answer her questions honestly. She may have questions, maybe immediately, maybe later. Answer them truthfully. If you don't know or don't remember, say so honestly rather than guessing.

Don't make it about you. If you start to cry or feel overwhelmed, that's understandable, but don't let your feelings take over the room. She shouldn't end up comforting you about your guilt. If you need a moment to compose yourself, take it, but return the focus to her.

After Disclosure

In the period after Disclosure, she is very vulnerable. She'll need time and space to process what she's heard. This might mean:

- Giving her physical space if she needs it
- Not pressing for reassurance about the relationship
- Being available to answer questions if she has them
- Managing your own feelings with your therapist and support network, not with her
- Continuing your recovery work with even more commitment

She may be angry, devastated, numb, or some combination. She may need days or weeks to process.

Whatever her response, respect it. You've just confirmed her worst fears about your behavior. She gets to feel whatever she feels.

Your job now is to demonstrate, through consistent actions over time, that the person who showed up for Disclosure (honest, accountable, focused on her needs) is who you're becoming, not just who you were for that one conversation.

Back to You: Protecting Yourself During Disclosure

Disclosure will be difficult. Here are some things that can help you navigate it:

Have your own support present. Your therapist should be there, or at least available immediately afterward. You need someone whose only job is to support you through this.

Know that you can take breaks. If you're overwhelmed, you can pause. You can ask for a few minutes. This isn't a marathon you must complete in one sitting.

Prepare for physical and emotional reactions. You might feel sick, shaky, enraged, numb, or all of these. You might dissociate: feel like you're watching from outside yourself. These are normal trauma responses. Let your therapist know your concerns so they can watch for signs you're struggling and help you through it.

You don't have to respond immediately. After Disclosure, you might need time (hours, days, weeks) to process what you've heard. You don't have to know what you think or feel right away. You don't have to make any decisions.

Consider practical arrangements. Think ahead about the hours and days after Disclosure. How will you get home: separately or together? Where will you each sleep that night? Do you want to be alone or have someone with you? Who can you call? Having some plans in place reduces the number of decisions you need to make when you're depleted.

What to Notice

As you experience Disclosure, pay attention to what you observe. Not to grade him, but to gather information for your own reflection:

Does it feel complete? Or do you sense there's more he's not saying? You've developed good instincts about when he's hiding something. Trust them.

Is he taking responsibility? Or do you hear subtle blame-shifting, minimizing, or excuses creeping in?

Can he stay present with your pain? Or does he collapse into his own guilt, start defending himself, or try to manage your emotions?

Does his remorse feel genuine? Is he sorry for what he did to you, or mainly sorry about the consequences for himself?

How does your body respond? When he speaks, what do you feel physically? Our bodies often know things before our minds process them.

You don't need to analyze all this in the moment. Just notice. Let your observations settle. They'll become clearer over time and will help you as you reflect on both **Question One** (Is genuine change happening?) and **Question Four** (Is there enough foundation to rebuild?).

After Disclosure

The period immediately after Disclosure is tender and requires care.

Take care of yourself first. You've just absorbed a lot of painful information. Ground yourself however you can: a walk, a bath, time with a supportive friend, whatever helps you feel steady. Drink water. Eat something if you can. Be very gentle with yourself.

Let your feelings be what they are. You might feel devastated, relieved that you finally know, furious, strangely calm, or some combination. All of it is normal. Don't judge yourself for however you're responding.

Don't make any big decisions yet. You're in no state to decide anything about your future right now. Give yourself time to process before drawing conclusions.

Know that more processing will come. You'll likely have questions that arise later, things you want clarified, emotions that surface over the following days and weeks. That's expected and okay.

Reach out to your support system. Call the trusted friend. Go to your therapy appointment. Attend your support group meeting. Don't isolate with this pain.

He needs support too, but not from you. This is important. He may be shaken by what he's confessed, flooded with shame, uncertain about what happens now. But managing his feelings is not your job. His therapist, sponsor, and recovery community should be supporting him through this. You have enough to carry.

Sophie's Disclosure Experience

Sophie dreaded Disclosure. In the weeks leading up to it, she could barely eat. She imagined the worst possibilities and tormented herself with scenarios.

The day itself was surreal. She sat in my office, hands shaking, as her husband, Nathan, read from his prepared statement. The scope of his behavior was worse than she'd imagined: multiple affairs, thousands of dollars on escorts, years of lying.

"I remember feeling like I was underwater," she told me later. "Like everything was muffled and far away. I heard the words, but I couldn't quite process them. I think my brain was protecting me by not letting it fully land."

That night, Sophie stayed at her sister's house. She didn't sleep. She cried until she had no tears left, then lay in the dark feeling strangely empty.

"The next few days were some of the worst of my life," she said. "But also, and I know this sounds strange, there was something almost like relief mixed in. Because I finally knew. I wasn't wondering anymore. The truth was horrible, but at least it was the truth."

Over the following weeks, Sophie had many more questions. She and Nathan had follow-up conversations, facilitated by professional help, to clarify details and fill in gaps. Each conversation was painful, but each also added to her sense of finally understanding what she was dealing with.

"Before Disclosure, I felt crazy," she said. "I knew something

was wrong, but I couldn't prove it, and he kept making me feel like I was imagining things. After Disclosure, I didn't feel crazy anymore. Devastated, yes. But not crazy. The reality finally matched what my gut had been telling me."

A Word About Incomplete Disclosure

Sometimes partners sense that they haven't received the full truth, that there's more being held back.

If you feel this way, take it seriously. Trust your gut.

You can say: "I don't feel like I've heard everything. I need you to go back to your therapist, do more work on this, and make sure you've been completely honest. Because I can't make decisions about my life based on partial information."

A partner who is genuinely committed to recovery will receive this as an opportunity to do better. He might be defensive in the moment, but he'll ultimately go back and do the work.

A partner who dismisses your concerns, insists you're being paranoid, or turns it around on you is showing you something important. Complete honesty may not be something he's capable of, at least not yet.

When Disclosure Reveals Deal-Breakers

Sometimes what you learn in Disclosure changes everything. You might discover:

- Behaviors that feel like absolute deal-breakers to you
- Betrayals involving people you know, which feel

qualitatively different

- A scope or duration that's far beyond what you'd imagined
- Health risks and financial misappropriation that mean you need to fundamentally reconsider everything
- Patterns that reveal something about who he is that you can't accept

If Disclosure reveals something that feels like a deal-breaker, you don't have to decide anything immediately. But you also don't have to override your response. If your gut says "I can't come back from this," that's important information.

This doesn't mean you must immediately leave. But it might mean the question has shifted from "Can we rebuild?" to "Can I ever accept this?" Give yourself time to sit with whatever Disclosure has revealed before pushing yourself toward any particular conclusion.

When you're ready, the next chapter guides you in preparing your Impact Letter: your opportunity to speak your truth about how his addiction has affected you.

5. Your Impact Letter

Speaking Your Truth

At some point after Disclosure, there is an important process called an Impact Letter, where you get to speak: to tell your partner, in your own words, how his addiction and betrayal have affected you. Your Impact Letter is a powerful opportunity for your voice to be heard.

Why the Impact Letter Matters

You've been carrying so much. The shock of discovery, the pain of betrayal, the exhausting work of trying to make sense of what happened. You've felt things you may never have felt before: rage, grief, fear, disgust, shame, confusion.

The Impact Letter gives you space to express all of it.

But it's not just about venting. It's about being witnessed. It's about your partner hearing, really hearing, what his choices have cost you. It's about you having the experience of speaking your truth and having it received.

For many partners, the Impact Letter is a turning point. Not because it fixes anything, but because something shifts when you finally get to say, out loud, to the person who hurt you, exactly what his behavior has done to you. When you stop protecting him from the truth of your pain and let him see it fully.

How he receives your Impact Letter is also revealing.

Can he listen without defending himself? Can he sit with your pain without making it about his guilt? Does he truly absorb what you're saying, or is he just waiting for it to be over?

This isn't about punishing him. It's about truth-telling, and truth-telling is essential for any possibility of healing, whether you stay together or not.

Kim's Impact Letter

Kim had been holding in her feelings for months. She was so focused on managing the crisis, dealing with practical matters, researching addiction, experiencing Disclosure, monitoring her husband's recovery, that she hadn't fully let herself feel her own pain.

Writing her Impact Letter broke something open in her.

"I sat down thinking I'd write a page or two," she told me. "I wrote twelve pages. I didn't know I had that much inside me. But once I started, it just poured out: all the anger, all the sadness, all the ways my life had been affected that I hadn't even consciously acknowledged."

Kim wrote about the night she'd found the messages on his phone. About lying awake wondering who he was texting when he said he was working late. About looking at their wedding photos and feeling nauseated. About not being able to enjoy sex because she kept wondering if he was thinking about someone else. About snapping at her kids because she had no reserves left. About the weight loss, the insomnia, the constant anxiety humming beneath the surface of her life.

"Writing it all down made me realize how much I'd been carrying," she said. "And how much I'd been minimizing. I kept telling myself it wasn't that bad, I was handling it. But seeing it all written out—the scope of the damage—I couldn't pretend anymore."

When Kim read her letter to her husband, something shifted between them.

"He cried," she said. "Not the defensive crying where he's feeling sorry for himself. Real crying. Like he was finally, for the first time, actually seeing what he'd done to me. He kept saying, 'I didn't know. I didn't know it was this bad.' And I thought, of course you didn't know. Because I was protecting you from knowing. I was carrying all of this alone."

Kim isn't sure if her marriage will survive. But she knows that reading her Impact Letter was essential, not for the marriage but for herself.

"I needed to say it. I needed him to hear it. Whatever happens next, I needed that."

What Might Go Into Your Impact Letter

There's no formula for this. Your Impact Letter should reflect your actual experience, whatever that is. But it might help to think about different areas of your life that have been affected:

Emotional impact. How has this affected your feelings: about him, about yourself, about your relationship, about life in general? What emotions have you experienced since discovery? What emotions do you live with daily now?

Impact on trust. How has your ability to trust been affected: trust in him, trust in others, trust in yourself? Do you question your own judgment now? Your perceptions? Your worth?

Physical impact. Has the stress affected your body? Sleep problems, appetite changes, weight fluctuations, headaches, illness, exhaustion? Has your health been directly put at risk?

Impact on the relationship. How has this changed how you see your relationship, your history together, your future? What do you grieve? What has been lost that can never be recovered?

Impact on intimacy. How has this affected your ability to be close to him, emotionally, physically, sexually? What does intimacy feel like now? What triggers you? What feels contaminated?

Impact on daily life. How has this affected your ability to work, parent, maintain friendships, engage with your community? How much time and energy has this consumed? What have you had to put aside?

Impact on your sense of self. How has this affected your identity, your confidence, your sense of who you are in the world? Do you feel diminished? Uncertain? Like you don't know yourself anymore?

Impact on your sense of safety. Do you feel safe in this relationship? In your home? In your own skin? What does it mean to live with someone who has proven capable of this level of deception?

Impact on your faith or worldview. Has this affected your spiritual life, your beliefs about the world, your sense of meaning or hope? Has it shaken foundations you thought were solid?

Impact on your future. How has this affected your dreams, your plans, your sense of what's possible? What possibilities have been lost? What fears have been created?

Writing Your Letter

There's no right way or correct timeline to write your Impact Letter. Some partners write pages and pages; others write a few paragraphs. Some organize it by theme; others let it flow as it comes. What matters is that it's honest and that it's yours.

Write for yourself first. Don't worry about how it sounds or whether it's "fair." This isn't a legal document where you need to present both sides. This is your truth, your experience, your pain. Let it be what it is.

Don't censor yourself. If you're furious, let the fury be there. If you hate him right now, say so. If you feel ugly, shameful thoughts you've never voiced, this is the place to voice them. You can always edit later, but first drafts should be uncensored.

Be specific when that helps. General statements like "you hurt me" are true but less powerful than specifics: "When I found out you spent our anniversary texting her, something broke in me. That dinner I thought was so romantic, you were lying to me the whole time." Specific moments carry weight.

Use "I" statements. "I felt . . ." "I experienced . . ." "I struggle with . . ." This keeps the focus on your experience rather than becoming an attack he feels he needs to defend against. You can express tremendous pain and anger through "I" statements.

Give yourself time. You don't have to write this in one sitting. Let it evolve over days or weeks. New thoughts will emerge. Things you didn't realize you were carrying will surface.

Revise as many times as you need. This letter is for you to share when you're ready. Take your time with it.

Amanda's Writing Process

Amanda struggled to start her Impact Letter. Every time she sat down to write, she'd stare at the blank page and feel overwhelmed.

"I didn't know where to begin," she said. "There was so much. It felt like trying to describe an ocean when someone asks about the water."

I suggested she not try to write the whole thing at once. Instead, I asked her to just write about one specific moment: the moment she found out.

"I can do that," she said.

That one moment became two pages. And once those pages were written, other moments followed. The day she had to get an STD test. The night she couldn't stop her hands from shaking. The conversation with her sister where she finally admitted what was happening. The way she flinches now when his phone buzzes.

"I realized I didn't need to explain the whole ocean," Amanda said. "I just needed to describe the waves. One wave at a time. And eventually, there was enough there that you could see what the ocean was."

Amanda's approach (starting small, with specifics, and letting the larger picture emerge) works for many partners. If you're stuck, try writing about just one moment, one experience, one feeling. Then another. The letter will build.

Preparing to Present Your Letter

When you're ready to share your letter with your partner, here are some things to consider:

Have support present. Your therapist, his therapist, or both should be there. You need someone focused on your well-being who can help if you become overwhelmed or if the conversation goes off the rails.

Set expectations beforehand. He should understand that his job is to listen, not to defend, explain, or respond in the moment. He can ask clarifying questions if something isn't clear, but this is about him receiving your truth, not about dialogue.

Take your time. Read at whatever pace feels right. Pause when you need to. Let yourself feel what you feel.

You don't owe him comfort. If he's distressed by what he hears, that's appropriate. He should be distressed. He's hearing the damage he's caused. It's not your job to make him feel better about it. If he falls apart, his therapist can help him manage that.

You can stop if you need to. If it becomes too much, you can take a break or continue another time.

His Role in Receiving Your Letter

When you present your Impact Letter, your partner's job is simple but not easy: to listen, receive, and witness your pain without defending himself.

He should not:

- Interrupt to explain or correct details
- Defend himself or his behavior
- Minimize what you're describing
- Try to manage your emotions ("Calm down," "Don't get so upset")
- Make it about himself ("I'm such a terrible person")
- Ask for reassurance or forgiveness
- Promise to make it better

He should:

- Listen fully, giving you his complete attention
- Let your words land
- Tolerate the discomfort of witnessing your pain
- Stay present even when it's hard
- Accept responsibility for what he's hearing
- Trust that whatever you're feeling is valid

This is difficult for most addicts. They've spent years avoiding difficult emotions, their own and others'. Sitting with someone's pain without trying to fix, deflect, or escape is not a skill they've developed.

But it's essential. Your pain exists because of his behavior. He needs to witness it without being protected from it.

Pages to Share With Your Partner: Receiving the Impact Letter

The following section is written directly to your partner. You can share it with him if you think it would help him understand what you need:

Your partner is preparing to share her Impact Letter with you: a detailed, honest account of how your addiction and betrayal have affected her life.

This will be hard to hear. But it's essential that you hear it well.

Why This Matters

Your partner has been carrying the weight of your behavior. Not just the betrayal itself, but all its ripple effects through her life. Her sleep, her health, her sense of self, her ability to trust, her relationships, her work, her faith, everything has been touched by what you did.

She needs you to understand this. Not intellectually, but truly. She needs to see that her pain has registered with you, that you grasp the full scope of the damage.

She also needs to speak her truth and be heard. She's been managing, coping, getting through, often while protecting you from the full weight of how she's really been affected. Now it's time for her to stop protecting you and let you see it.

Your One Job: Listen

When she reads her letter, your job is simple: Listen. Receive. Witness.

That's it. You don't need to say the right thing. You don't need to fix anything. You just need to be fully present, taking in what she's sharing.

This is harder than it sounds. Everything in you will want to defend yourself, explain, apologize, make it better. You'll want to say, "But I was struggling too" or "I never meant to hurt you" or "I'm not that person anymore."

Don't. Not now.

Now is for listening. You'll have opportunities to respond later. But this moment is about her being heard.

What to Expect

Her letter might include things that are difficult to hear:

- The depth and scope of pain you've caused
- How your behavior has affected every area of her life
- Anger, hatred, disgust: intense feelings directed at you
- Grief for what she's lost
- Fear about whether she can ever feel safe with you
- Questioning of your entire relationship history

All of this is valid. Even if it's hard to hear. Even if it feels unfair. Even if you're not the same person who did those things.

You did cause this damage. She's telling you what it cost her. She gets to tell it however she needs to.

Managing Your Own Feelings

You'll have feelings while she reads it. Shame, guilt, grief, defensiveness, maybe even anger. These are natural but must not take over the room.

This is not about you. This is about her.

If you feel yourself getting overwhelmed, take a breath. Ground yourself. Remember why you're here: to finally let her be seen and heard.

If you need to cry, that's okay; tears that are about truly feeling the impact of your actions can be appropriate. But don't collapse into your own pain in a way that requires her to take care of you.

If you start to feel defensive, notice it and let it go. You'll have time to share your perspective later. Right now, your only job is to receive hers.

After She Reads

When she finishes, you don't need to have the perfect response.

You can simply say:

- "Thank you for sharing that with me."
- "I hear you. I'm so sorry for the pain I've caused."

- "I had no idea the full extent of how this affected you. Thank you for helping me understand."

Don't:

- Immediately apologize at length (this can feel like trying to make yourself feel better)
- Ask what happens now (let her lead)
- Seek reassurance about the relationship
- Defend yourself or clarify any details
- Say "I understand" (you can't fully understand; "I hear you" is better)

In the days that follow, she may have more to say, more questions, more feelings that emerge. Be available, be patient, and keep listening.

The Empathy Response

Later, you'll have an opportunity to respond more fully, to show her that you truly understand and feel the impact of your behavior. This is called the Empathy Response, and we'll discuss it in the next chapter.

For now, just focus on receiving her Impact Letter fully. That means listening with your whole self, letting her pain matter to you, and resisting every urge to defend or deflect.

This is one of the most important things you can do in your recovery. It's not about earning forgiveness or saving your relationship. It's about finally, fully acknowledging what you've done and what it's cost the person you claim to love.

Back to You: What to Notice

As you share your Impact Letter and witness his response, pay attention to what you observe and feel:

Do you feel heard? Not perfectly understood (that may not be possible) but genuinely heard? Does it seem like your words are landing?

Is he present? Is he really there with you, or does he seem distant, checked out, waiting for it to be over?

Does he stay in his seat? Emotionally speaking, does he stay present with your pain? Or does he collapse into his own guilt, start defending himself, or try to manage your emotions?

How does your body feel? After sharing, do you feel a sense of relief, even amid the pain? Or do you feel more depleted, like the words didn't land where they needed to?

What does your gut say? About him, about whether genuine understanding is present, about whether this process is helping?

These observations will inform:

Question One (Is genuine change happening?): Specifically, can he develop real empathy? And **Question Four** (Is there enough foundation?): Specifically, can he truly hear you?.

When you're ready, the next chapter explores the Empathy Response, his opportunity to show you that he truly understands and feels what his behavior has cost you.

6. The Empathy Response

Can He Truly See You?

After you've shared your Impact Letter, the next step in the process gives your partner an opportunity to respond: not with explanations or defenses, but with empathy. He tries to show you that he's heard you, that he understands what his addiction has cost you, that he truly grasps the depth of your pain.

This is called the Empathy Response, and it's one of the most revealing moments in his recovery process.

Why Empathy Matters So Much

Empathy is the ability to feel with someone: to truly understand their experience, not just acknowledge it intellectually. For genuine intimacy to exist in a relationship, both partners need to be capable of empathy.

In healthy relationships, empathy happens naturally. When one partner is hurt, the other feels something too. When one shares good news, the other shares the joy. There's a resonance, a being-with, that creates connection.

Sex addiction damages this capacity.

Addicts typically spend years numbing their emotions, disconnecting from their own feelings as well as others'. They become skilled at compartmentalization, keeping their acting-out separate from their "real" life. This disconnection often extends to their partners. They can hurt you while somehow not fully registering that they're hurting you.

Recovery requires developing the capacity for empathy.

This is deep work, and it doesn't happen overnight. But genuine recovery will include a growing ability to truly see you, feel your pain, and understand the impact of his choices.

The Empathy Response shows you where he is in this process.

Can he move beyond his shame and guilt to actually focus on your experience? Can he demonstrate understanding of what you've been through? Or does he collapse into his own feelings, leaving you once again feeling unseen?

The Difference Between Empathy and Guilt

Many addicts confuse guilt with empathy. They feel terrible about what they've done, and they assume this means they understand their partner's pain.

But guilt and empathy are different:

Guilt is about him. It's focused on his feelings about his behavior, his shame, his sense of being a bad person. Guilt says, "I feel terrible about myself because of what I did."

Empathy is about you. It's focused on understanding your experience, your pain, your world. Empathy says, "I can feel what this has been like for you. I understand how my behavior has affected your life."

When a partner shares his guilt, it often feels like more burden for you. Now you have to manage his feelings about his behavior. When a partner shares genuine empathy, it feels like being seen and understood.

You can tell the difference. Guilt leaves you feeling alone with your pain while also having to worry about him. Empathy makes you feel less alone, truly accompanied in your suffering.

Wendy's Experience

After Wendy read her Impact Letter to her husband Greg, he broke down sobbing.

"I'm such a terrible person," he kept saying. "I can't believe I did this to you. I hate myself. I don't deserve to live."

Wendy found herself comforting him. Telling him he wasn't a terrible person. Telling him it would be okay. And afterward, she felt empty and resentful.

"I was the one who was supposed to be heard," she told me. "But somehow it became about him. About his guilt, his self-hatred.

I ended up taking care of his feelings about hurting me. It's what I always do."

What Wendy received wasn't empathy: it was guilt. Greg's response was genuine in its way; he did feel terrible. But it was centered on his experience, not hers. Instead of making her feel seen, it made her feel responsible for managing his emotions.

I worked with Greg on understanding the difference. "Your guilt is real, and you'll need to work through it, with your therapist, with your sponsor, in your own reflection. But when Wendy shares her pain, she needs you to focus on her, not on how bad you feel about yourself."

Greg struggled with this. Focusing on Wendy's pain meant really feeling what he'd done to her, which was almost unbearable. It was easier to collapse into self-hatred than to stay present with her experience.

But over time, with practice, Greg developed more capacity for genuine empathy. His second attempt at an Empathy Response was different.

"I heard you describe lying awake at night, wondering where I was, wondering if you were crazy for doubting me," he said. "I did that to you. I made you question your own sanity. You were right to doubt me: your instincts were trying to protect you, and I made you feel like something was wrong with you for having them. That must have been so disorienting and lonely."

Wendy felt the difference immediately. "That one actually landed," she told me. "He wasn't talking about how bad he felt. He was talking about what I went through. It's the first time I've felt like he actually saw me."

What a Formal Empathy Response Includes

An Empathy Response should demonstrate that your partner has truly heard your Impact Letter, not just the words, but the meaning beneath them.

It should be specific. Not just "I know I hurt you," but evidence that he's taken in the particular ways you've been affected. He should reference specific things from your letter, showing that he heard and absorbed them.

It should focus on your experience. Not on his guilt, his reasons, his feelings about himself. On you. What you went through. What you're still going through.

It should validate your feelings. "Your anger makes sense. Your grief makes sense. What you're feeling isn't an overreaction, it's a completely appropriate response to what I did."

It should take full responsibility. Clean accountability without excuses, without "but," without minimizing.

It should express genuine sorrow. Not "I'm sorry you're hurt" (which subtly makes it about your reaction) but "I'm sorry for what I did to you" (which owns the cause).

It should make no demands. A genuine Empathy Response doesn't ask for forgiveness, reassurance, or any particular response. It simply offers understanding and accountability.

What an Empathy Response Might Sound Like

Again, this isn't a script; it's an illustration of the spirit of what genuine empathy sounds like:

"I've spent a lot of time with your Impact Letter. Not just reading it, but really trying to feel what you've been living with.

"I heard you describe the night you found the messages. The way your hands shook. The way the world tilted and nothing felt real. I did that to you. I shattered your sense of reality with my lies.

"I heard you describe lying awake wondering if you were crazy, feeling like something was wrong but being told everything was fine. I gaslit you for years. Every time you asked a question and I made you feel paranoid, I was choosing to protect my addiction instead of honoring your perceptions. You weren't crazy. You were right. And I stole your ability to trust yourself.

"I heard you describe not being able to look at our wedding photos without feeling sick. I contaminated those memories. You don't know anymore what was real and what was performance. That must feel like losing your history, like not having a solid foundation of truth to stand on.

"I heard you describe how this has affected your body: the weight loss, the insomnia, the constant anxiety humming beneath everything. My behavior put your nervous system into crisis. Your body has been paying the price for my behavior.

"I heard you describe feeling like you weren't enough, not attractive enough, not interesting enough. I need you to know: my addiction had nothing to do with anything lacking in you. You

were always more than enough. The problem was entirely mine, my broken coping mechanisms, my inability to be present with real intimacy. None of this was about your adequacy.

"I heard your rage, and it makes complete sense. I deserve it. I betrayed you in the most fundamental way while looking you in the eye and telling you everything was fine. You have every right to be furious.

"I can't undo what I've done. But I want you to know that I've heard you. Your pain is real, it matters, and I caused it. I'm not asking for anything from you. I just want you to know that I see what I did, and I see what it cost you."

Why Empathy Is Hard for Addicts

Understanding why empathy is difficult for many addicts can help you interpret what you're seeing, not to excuse inadequate empathy but to recognize what genuine effort looks like given where he's starting from.

Many addicts didn't receive empathy as children. They grew up in environments where their feelings weren't recognized or valued. They never learned to attune to others because no one attuned to them.

Addiction requires emotional disconnection. To continue hurting someone you love while pretending everything is fine, you have to disconnect from feeling. Years of this practice atrophies the empathy muscle.

Shame blocks empathy. When shame is overwhelming, it's hard to focus on anyone else's experience. Shame screams so loudly that it drowns out the ability to feel with another person.

Empathy requires feeling. If he's spent years numbing his feelings, accessing genuine emotion—including empathic emotion—is genuinely difficult. It's like asking someone who hasn't walked in years to run a marathon.

This doesn't mean empathy is impossible. It means it has to be developed, often for the first time. Here's what's important to understand: Many people can't feel genuine empathy for others until they've learned to feel empathy for themselves, particularly for the wounded child they once were, the child that discovered sexual behavior and fantasy as a way to stifle his pain.

Genuine recovery includes this emotional growth. Through trauma treatment, he begins to develop compassion for his own childhood experiences of abuse and neglect. As he learns to see that child with empathy rather than shame, he becomes capable of seeing you, and the pain he's caused you, with genuine empathy as well. This is why his Empathy Response may come later in recovery rather than immediately. The capacity has to be built first.

What you're watching for is effort and trajectory. Is he trying to understand your experience, even if imperfectly? Is his capacity for empathy growing over time? Is he doing the therapeutic work to develop it?

An addict who acknowledges his empathy limitations, is actively working on them, and shows genuine effort in his response is very different from one who remains emotionally shut down or makes everything about his own feelings.

Darlene's Experience

Darlene's husband Alan struggled with the Empathy Response. His first attempt was stilted and wooden: clearly prepared, but without real feeling behind it. It felt like he was reading a script rather than actually connecting with her experience.

Darlene told him so. "That didn't feel real," she said. "I don't feel like you actually understand. It felt like you were performing."

Alan was frustrated. "I'm trying," he said. "I did everything my therapist told me to. What more do you want?"

This response told Darlene something important: Alan was approaching this as a task to complete, not as a genuine attempt to connect with her pain. He wanted credit for trying, not feedback on how to do better.

But Alan kept working on it. His therapist helped him understand that empathy couldn't be faked. He had to actually feel something, not just say the right words. They worked on helping Alan access his own emotions, which had been shut down for decades.

His second attempt, weeks later, was different. Less polished, more halting, but more real.

"I keep thinking about what you said about our anniversary dinner," he said, his voice catching. "How you thought it was so special, and I was texting her under the table. I can see you there, happy, thinking we were having this beautiful moment, and I was . . . God, I was lying to your face. You deserved so much better than that. You deserved an actual partner, not whatever I was

pretending to be."

Darlene felt the difference. "That one was real," she said. "Not perfect, but real. I could tell you were actually feeling something, not just saying what you thought you should say."

Alan's empathy was still developing. But Darlene could see trajectory. He was growing, not just performing. That mattered more than perfection.

What to Notice

As you witness your partner's Empathy Response, pay attention:

Does it feel genuine? Can you sense real feeling behind the words, or does it feel like performance?

Is it focused on you? Or does it keep drifting back to his guilt, his shame, his feelings about himself?

Is it specific? Does he reference actual things from your Impact Letter or is it generic?

How does your body respond? Do you feel more seen, more understood? Or do you feel alone, unsatisfied, like the words missed you somehow?

What does your gut say? You know him. You can sense the difference between genuine feeling and going through the motions.

These observations directly inform:

Question One (Is genuine change happening?): Specifically, is empathy developing? And **Question Four** (Is there enough foundation?): Specifically, can he truly see and feel with you?

When Empathy Falls Short

Sometimes the Empathy Response doesn't land. It might be too generic, too focused on his feelings, too defensive, or simply empty of real emotion.

If this happens, you have options:

Name what's missing. "I don't feel heard. Your response felt like it was more about your guilt than about my experience. I need you to try again."

Give him time to develop. Empathy doesn't develop overnight, especially for someone starting from a significant deficit. If he's genuinely working on it and showing incremental progress, that might be enough to encourage him to keep working on it.

Recognize what this tells you. If, after genuine effort and time, empathy remains absent, that's important information. Intimacy requires two people who can feel with each other. If he can't get there, the relationship may not be able to become what you need it to be.

Pages to Share With Your Partner: Preparing the Empathy Response

The following section is written directly to your partner. You can share it with him if you think it would help him understand what you need.

Your partner has shared her Impact Letter with you. Now she needs something more than acknowledgment. She needs to know you truly understand and feel what your behavior has cost her.

This is called the Empathy Response, and it may be one of the most challenging things you do in recovery, not because the task is complicated but because it requires genuine emotional connection that you may not have practiced before.

Understanding What's Needed

Your partner doesn't need to hear how bad you feel about yourself. She's not asking for guilt, shame, or self-flagellation. She needs to know that you see her, that you understand her experience, her pain, her world.

The difference matters:

Guilt says: "I feel terrible about what I did."

Empathy says: "I can feel what this has been like for you."

Guilt is about you. **Empathy** is about her.

When you share your guilt, she often ends up having to take care of your feelings, reassuring you that you're not a terrible person, managing your emotional response. That's the opposite of what she needs.

When you share genuine empathy, she feels seen and understood. Less alone. Like her pain matters and has registered with you.

How to Prepare

Go back to her Impact Letter. Read it again, slowly. Not to prepare a response, but to really take it in. As you read, try to imagine her experience. Not just intellectually. Actually feel your way into it, as if this these same things had happened to you.

- What was it like for her to discover your betrayal?
- What has it been like for her to live with the aftermath?
- How has it affected her daily life, her sense of self, her ability to trust?
- What has she lost?
- What does she fear?

Let yourself feel something. Not guilt about being a bad person, but feeling about what she's gone through. This might be uncomfortable. You've probably spent years avoiding feelings. But empathy requires feeling.

Work with your therapist on this. Practice articulating what you understand about her experience. Notice when you drift into guilt ("I'm such a terrible person") and redirect to empathy ("She must have felt so alone when . . .”).

What Your Response Should Include

When you deliver your Empathy Response, it should:

Be specific. Reference particular things from her letter. Show her you actually heard and absorbed what she shared.

Focus on her experience. Not on your feelings about yourself. On what she went through.

Validate her feelings. Let her know that her anger, grief, fear, whatever she experienced, makes complete sense.

Take responsibility. Clean ownership without excuses or explanations.

Express genuine sorrow. Sorrow for what you did to her, not just sorrow about being a bad person.

Make no demands. Don't ask for forgiveness, reassurance, or any particular response.

What It Might Sound Like

"I've been sitting with your letter, really trying to understand what you've been living with.

"[Reference specific things from her letter, showing you absorbed them]

"I can only imagine how [describe her experience with genuine feeling]. You were [validate her response]. That makes complete sense.

"I did this to you. My behavior caused this pain. There's no excuse, no explanation that makes it okay.

"I'm deeply sorry for what I've put you through. Not just the behavior itself, but all the ways it's rippled through your life—[name specific impacts she described].

"I'm not asking for anything. I just want you to know that I've heard you, that I understand as much as I'm able to, and that your pain matters to me."

Common Pitfalls to Avoid

Making it about your guilt. If you find yourself talking about how terrible you feel, redirect to her experience.

Defending or explaining. No "but I was struggling too" or "I never meant to hurt you." Clean accountability only.

Generic responses. "I know I hurt you" isn't enough. Show her you heard the specific ways.

Seeking reassurance. Don't end with questions about the relationship or requests for forgiveness.

Performing instead of feeling. She'll know the difference. If you're just saying words without feeling, it won't land.

If You Struggle with Empathy

If empathy is genuinely difficult for you (and for many addicts it is) be honest about that.

You can say: "I want you to know that I'm struggling to access the kind of emotional understanding you deserve. It's not because your pain doesn't matter. It's because I've spent so long disconnected from feelings that this is genuinely hard for me. I'm working on it with my therapist. I'm committed to developing this capacity, even though I'm not there yet."

This kind of honesty, acknowledging your limitations while committing to growth, is better than performing empathy you don't actually feel.

What she most needs to see is that you're trying, that you're growing, and that her pain genuinely matters to you. Perfect empathy isn't required. Genuine effort and trajectory are.

Back to You: After the Empathy Response

After witnessing his Empathy Response, give yourself time to process.

Notice what you feel. Did it help? Do you feel more seen? Or does something still feel missing?

Trust your gut. You know whether it felt real or performed. You know whether you feel more connected or still alone.

It doesn't have to be perfect. Especially if empathy is genuinely difficult for him, imperfect but genuine effort can be meaningful. What matters is whether you sense he's truly trying and whether there's growth over time.

This is information, not verdict. The Empathy Response gives you data about his capacity for emotional connection. It's one piece of the picture, not the whole picture.

When you're ready, the next chapter explores the Transparency Agreement: creating structures for ongoing honesty and accountability.

7. The Transparency Agreement

Can Honesty Become the New Normal?

As recovery progresses, you'll need some way to structure ongoing honesty and accountability. This is where a Transparency Agreement comes in: a set of shared understandings about how your partner will maintain openness going forward.

Why Transparency Matters

Secrecy was the fuel for addiction. Your partner built a hidden life, maintained elaborate deceptions, and created compartments you never knew existed. The addiction thrived in darkness.

Recovery requires the opposite: living openly, with nothing hidden.

Transparency isn't about controlling him. It's not about you becoming his parole officer or babysitter. It's about creating conditions where trust can possibly be rebuilt.

Think about it: After what you've experienced, how could you begin to trust again based only on his word? His word has proven unreliable. You believed him before, and he was lying.

Transparency provides verification while trust is being rebuilt. It's scaffolding: a temporary structure that supports the building process until the building is strong enough to stand on its own. Eventually, if recovery is genuine and trust is restored, you won't need the same level of transparency. But for now, you need to be able to verify rather than simply believe.

How he responds to transparency tells you a lot. Does he understand why it's necessary and accept it willingly? Or does he resist, resent it, call it controlling, look for ways around it?

A partner in genuine recovery gets it. He understands that he destroyed trust and that rebuilding it requires more than promises. He accepts transparency not as punishment but as a necessary part of healing what he broke.

What Transparency Might Include

Every couple's transparency agreement will look different, depending on their specific situation and needs. Here are some common elements:

Unlocked devices and accounts. Phones, computers, tablets, all accessible to you. Passwords shared. No secret accounts, hidden apps, or private browsing that you can't see if you want to. This doesn't mean you have to check constantly. But you can if you need to. The openness itself is what matters.

Location sharing. Many couples use location-sharing apps during recovery. Not so you can monitor his every move obsessively, but so there are no mysterious whereabouts. He's where he says he is, and you can see that.

Disclosure of slips or struggles. If he has a slip (any return to addiction behavior), you need to know. The agreement should specify how quickly he needs to tell you (usually within 24-48 hours) and what information you need.

Beyond slips, he should share when he's struggling: when he's triggered, when he's having a hard day, when his addiction is calling to him. Not so you can fix it, but so you're not in the dark about his internal state.

Recovery activity transparency. Is he attending meetings? In contact with his sponsor? Going to therapy? You should be able to know this without having to ask constantly or take his word for it.

Financial transparency. Full access to accounts. No secret credit cards or hidden spending. Visibility into where money goes.

Check-in rhythms. Regular times to talk about how recovery is going, how you're both feeling, what's working and what isn't. Not crisis conversations, but routine connection about the process you're both in.

Protocols for concerns. What happens if you're worried about something? How do you raise concerns? How does he respond? Having an agreed-upon process helps when things get tense.

Creating Your Agreement

The Transparency Agreement should be developed collaboratively, ideally with professional guidance. But "collaboratively" doesn't mean your needs take a back seat.

Your needs take priority. You're the one whose trust was shattered. You get to determine what you need to feel safe. He needs to work with those needs, not complain or try to negotiate them away.

Be specific. Vague agreements don't work. "I'll be more open" isn't an agreement. "I'll share my phone location through [specific app], and you'll have passwords to all devices and accounts" is.

Write it down. Having a written agreement creates clarity and prevents misunderstandings later.

Include what happens if agreements are broken. Not as threats, but as clarity. If he violates the transparency agreement, what are the consequences? Knowing this in advance prevents scrambling in the moment.

Examples might include:

- "If you delete browsing history or hide financial transactions, I will take a two-week separation to reassess whether I can continue in this relationship."
- "If you lie about your whereabouts or activities, couples therapy pauses until you've addressed this with your individual therapist and sponsor."

- "If you access pornography, our planned vacation is postponed until you've had 90 days of renewed sobriety."
- "If transparency violations occur, any major relationship decisions (moving in together, marriage, having children) are put on hold for at least six months."

These aren't punishments, they're protective boundaries that give you space to evaluate whether recovery is real and whether you feel safe continuing.

Expect to revise over time. What you need early in recovery might be different from what you need a year in. Some structures can be relaxed as trust rebuilds; others might need to be strengthened if problems emerge.

His Response to Transparency

Pay close attention to how your partner responds to the idea of transparency. This tells you something important about where he is in his recovery.

Healthy responses look like:

- "I understand why you need this. I broke your trust and I need to earn it back."
- "This makes sense. What do you need?"
- "I'm willing to do whatever it takes to help you feel safe."

- Accepting transparency without resentment or resistance
- Proactively offering transparency beyond what you ask

Concerning responses look like:

- "You're being controlling. Don't you trust me?"
- "How long do I have to do this? When can we go back to normal?"
- "This feels like punishment."
- Resistance, negotiation, or resentment
- Technically complying but finding loopholes
- Treating transparency as temporary inconvenience rather than necessary repair

A partner who bristles at transparency may not truly understand what he's done. He may still be thinking of this as a problem that happened rather than a betrayal he committed. He may be more focused on getting his privacy back than on rebuilding your trust.

Ruth's Transparency Journey

Ruth's husband James initially resisted transparency.

"He said I was being paranoid," Ruth told me. "He said if I couldn't trust him, what was the point? He made me feel like I was the one with the problem."

I helped Ruth understand that James's resistance was itself a problem. "A partner who gets why transparency is necessary doesn't fight it. He might not enjoy it, but he understands that he broke your trust and this is how it gets rebuilt."

Ruth held her ground. She explained to James that transparency wasn't optional. It was a requirement for her to even consider staying. She wasn't asking because she was controlling; she was asking because he'd proven his word wasn't enough.

James eventually agreed, but grudgingly. For the first few months, he complied with the letter of the agreement while subtly violating its spirit, sighing heavily when she checked his phone, making her feel guilty for using the location app.

"He was following the rules, but he wasn't really getting it," Ruth said. "It felt like he was just waiting me out until I stopped requiring it."

The turning point came in therapy, when James finally began to understand how his deception had affected Ruth. Something shifted when he really got it, when he felt the impact, not just acknowledged it intellectually.

"After that session, he came home and handed me his phone," Ruth said. "He said, 'I've been treating this like a burden. But you've been living with the burden of my lies for years. This is the least I can do.' Something in his tone was different. He wasn't resigned or resentful. He was . . . present."

Over time, Ruth found she needed to check less. Not because transparency ended, but because James's genuine embrace of it, rather than grudging compliance, allowed her nervous system to settle.

"I still have access to everything," she said. "But I don't feel the same desperate need to check constantly. Because I finally believe he wants me to know. He's not hiding anymore."

Living with Transparency

Transparency is a structure, but it's also a practice: something you live with daily.

For you:

- Check when you need to, without guilt. The access exists so you can use it.
- But notice if checking becomes compulsive, if you're unable to stop, unable to feel calm regardless of what you find. That might indicate you need more support or that something else is going on.
- Use the check-in rhythms to communicate about how you're feeling, what's helping, what's not.
- Allow transparency to evolve as trust rebuilds. Not prematurely, but genuinely as you feel more secure.

For him:

- Embrace transparency rather than tolerating it. The attitude matters as much as the compliance.
- Offer information proactively rather than waiting to be asked.
- Understand that her need to verify isn't personal insult, it's a trauma response to your betrayal.

- Stay committed even when it's inconvenient or uncomfortable.

What Transparency Reveals

As you live with your Transparency Agreement over weeks and months, pay attention to what it reveals:

Is he honoring it consistently? Not perfectly(everyone makes mistakes) but consistently? Are violations rare and immediately addressed, or are there patterns of slippage?

Is his attitude shifting? Does he increasingly understand why transparency matters or does he remain resentful?

Are you feeling safer over time? Not instantly, but gradually, is your sense of security growing?

Is he being proactive? Offering information before you ask? Telling you about struggles and triggers? Or are you still having to pull everything out of him?

These observations inform **Question Two** (Can I feel safe here?) And **Question Four** (Is there enough foundation?).

A partner who genuinely embraces transparency is building trust. A partner who fights, resents, or circumvents transparency is showing you that he hasn't fully accepted accountability for what he did.

When you're ready, the next chapter explores the quieter work of living with the **Five Questions** and letting clarity emerge over time.

8. Living in the Questions

Letting Clarity Emerge

You've been through intense experiences: the shock of discovery, the pain of Disclosure, the vulnerability of sharing your Impact Letter, the revealing moments of his Empathy Response, the ongoing practice of living with transparency.

Now comes a different kind of work: quieter, less dramatic, but equally important. It's the work of living with the Five Questions and letting clarity emerge over time.

There's No Deadline

You might feel pressure, from him, from others, from yourself, to know by now what you're going to do. Haven't you learned enough? Shouldn't you be able to decide?

But clarity can't be forced. It emerges in its own time, as you gather more information, do your own healing, and let the questions settle.

Some partners find clarity quickly. Within a few months of discovery, they know what they need to do. Others take a year or more. There's no right timeline. Only the timeline that leads you to a decision you can trust.

What you're looking for isn't certainty. You may never be 100% sure you're making the right choice. What you're looking for is clarity: knowing enough about yourself, your partner, and your situation to make a decision you can stand behind.

Clarity says: "I've seen what I needed to see. I know what I know. I may not know everything, but I know enough."

Watching Over Time

The recovery processes you've experienced (Disclosure, Impact Letters, Empathy Responses) were concentrated moments that revealed important things. But those moments don't tell the whole story.

Recovery reveals itself over time. Early efforts might be strong but then fade as the crisis recedes. Or initial struggles might give way to genuine growth as he gets more tools and does more work. You need to see how things unfold over weeks and months, not just in the intense moments.

Daily life is revealing. Beyond the formal processes, pay attention to ordinary moments:

- How does he handle stress? Does he reach for healthy coping or start to slip?
- Is he emotionally present? Or does he disappear into work, screens, emotional distance?
- Is honesty becoming natural? About small things as well as big ones?
- How does he respond when you're struggling? With patience and empathy, or with frustration and defensiveness?
- Is he doing recovery work consistently, or does it fade when pressure decreases?

Patterns matter more than snapshots. One bad day doesn't mean recovery is failing. One good week doesn't mean everything is fixed. What matters is the overall trajectory. Are things generally getting better, or is there a repeating cycle of effort and decline?

Checking In With Yourself

As you live with these questions, regularly check in with yourself about where you are:

What am I observing? Not what I hope or fear, but what do I actually see? What patterns are emerging?

What does my gut tell me? When I'm quiet and honest with myself, what do I sense about this relationship? About whether genuine change is happening?

Am I feeling safer over time? Is the trajectory toward more security, or less?

Can I imagine a future here? Not perfectly, not with complete certainty, but with some sense of possibility?

What do I need that I'm not getting? Are there essential things missing? Are they things that might develop, or are they things that seem impossible?

You might keep a journal to track these reflections over time. Not obsessive daily documentation, but periodic check-ins (maybe weekly or monthly) where you note where you are. These notes can reveal patterns and changes that are hard to see day to day.

Monica's Waiting Time

Monica struggled with the uncertainty of not knowing what she would do.

"Everyone keeps asking me," she said. "My mother, my friends, even people at work, they all want to know if I'm staying or leaving. And I don't know. I hate not knowing."

I assured Monica that not knowing was appropriate. She was in the middle of gathering information. She was healing from trauma. She was watching to see if her husband's recovery was real.

"You wouldn't decide to buy a house after one viewing," I said. "You'd look at it multiple times, get an inspection, think about it, sleep on it. This is a much bigger decision than buying a house. Of course it takes time."

Monica learned to sit with the uncertainty, not comfortably but without letting it drive her to premature decisions.

"What helped was realizing that not deciding was itself a decision," she said. "I was deciding to wait, to gather more information, to give myself time. That was the right decision for now."

Months later, Monica's clarity began to emerge. She noticed that her husband's recovery had remained steady. That her sense of safety had gradually grown. That she could imagine a future. Not the same future she'd imagined before, but a real one.

"I didn't have a lightning bolt moment where suddenly I knew," she said. "It was more like . . . the fog slowly lifting. Gradually I could see more clearly. And what I saw was: this might actually be possible."

Your Own Healing

While you're watching his recovery, you're also on your own healing journey. This work is essential, regardless of what you decide about the relationship.

Healing helps you see clearly. When you're in acute trauma, everything is colored by pain and fear. Your nervous system is in survival mode, not assessment mode. As you heal, you can evaluate more accurately.

Healing restores self-trust. Through the recovery process (and especially if you've been gaslit) you learn to trust your perceptions again. You learn that your gut is reliable, that your observations are accurate.

Healing clarifies your needs. As you recover from betrayal trauma, you get clearer about what you actually need to be well. Needs that seemed negotiable might reveal themselves as essential. Things you thought were dealbreakers might feel more manageable as you heal.

Healing is for you. Whatever happens with this relationship, your healing is yours. It will serve you whether you stay or go.

Therapy, Support, and Processing

During this living-with-the-questions period, continue your own therapeutic work:

Individual therapy gives you space to process what you're observing, work through trauma, and reconnect with yourself.

Support groups connect you with others on similar journeys, reminding you that you're not alone and offering perspectives you might not have considered.

Self-care remains essential. This is a marathon, not a sprint. You need to sustain yourself over the long period of uncertainty.

Trusted relationships matter. Keep people in your life who can hold space for your process without pushing you toward a particular outcome.

When Clarity Begins to Emerge

For many partners, there comes a point when the questions begin to answer themselves. Not all at once, but gradually. You notice:

Something settling. The desperate, churning uncertainty starts to quiet. Not because you've suppressed it, but because something is clarifying.

A direction becoming evident. When you imagine the future, one path starts to feel more real than the other.

Your gut speaking. That quiet inner voice that knows things, it begins to speak more clearly.

The questions having answers. Not perfect answers, not certain answers, but clear enough to act on.

This might happen in weeks. It might take much longer. There's no schedule for clarity.

When it begins to emerge, pay attention. Trust it. This is what you've been waiting for.

If You're Not There Yet

If clarity hasn't come, that's okay. It doesn't mean anything is wrong. It might mean:

You need more time. The situation hasn't evolved enough to reveal what you need to see. More patience is required.

You need more information. There are processes you haven't completed, questions you haven't asked, things you haven't observed that would help you know.

You need more healing. Sometimes clarity comes only after significant trauma healing. Your nervous system has to calm down enough for wisdom to emerge.

The situation is genuinely complicated. Some relationships fall into a gray zone where recovery is real but incomplete, where some needs are met but others aren't, where staying and leaving both have significant costs. These situations take longer to sort through.

Keep living with the questions. Keep doing your own work. Keep paying attention. The clarity will come when it's ready—and when you're ready.

When you're ready, the next chapter offers guidance for bringing everything together and making your decision.

9. Making Your Decision

Bringing It All Together

You've done significant work to arrive at this moment. You've weathered discovery, moved through painful processes, observed your partner's recovery efforts, done your own healing, and lived with the Five Questions over time.

Now you're ready, or close to ready, to bring it all together and make your decision.

This chapter offers a structured way to do that, drawing on everything you've learned and observed.

Revisiting the Questions

Find some quiet time, maybe a few hours spread across several days, to sit with each of the Five Questions and notice where you've landed.

Question One: Is genuine change happening?

Think about everything you've observed since discovery:

- How did he handle Disclosure? Was it complete, accountable, focused on you?
- How did he receive your Impact Letter?
- What was his Empathy Response like? Did it feel genuine?
- Has he been honoring the Transparency Agreement?
- What have you observed in daily life? Is he doing recovery work consistently?
- Is honesty becoming natural? Is his empathy growing?
- What's the trajectory: improving, stagnating, declining?

Sit with what you know

What does your honest assessment tell you about whether genuine change is happening?

Question Two: Can I feel safe here?

Think about your experience of safety in this relationship now:

- Can you express yourself without being punished or dismissed?
- Are your boundaries respected?

- Is transparency being maintained genuinely, not resentfully?
- Do you feel safer now than you did six months ago?
- What does your nervous system say? Can you relax, or are you still on constant alert?

Sit with what you know

What does your honest assessment tell you about whether safety is possible here?

Question Three: Can this relationship honor who I am?

Think about your core values and deepest needs:

- What do you need to feel truly fulfilled in a relationship?
- Are those needs being met? Can they be met here?
- Can you be your authentic self in this relationship?
- What would staying require you to accept or give up?
- Are there non-negotiables that are being violated?

Sit with what you know

What does your honest assessment tell you about whether this relationship can honor who you are?

Question Four: Is there enough foundation to build on?

Think about what exists beneath the addiction and betrayal:

- Is there genuine love, respect, friendship?
- Is he committed to building something new, not restoring something old?
- Is there enough good here to justify the massive effort of rebuilding?
- Do you have the resources, internal and external, for the long work ahead?

Sit with what you know

What does your honest assessment tell you about whether there's enough foundation?

Question Five: What does your deepest wisdom tell you?

After all the reflection, sit quietly with yourself:

- When you imagine staying and rebuilding, what do you feel in your body? In your heart?
- When you imagine leaving, what do you feel?
- What does your gut say?
- If you knew no one would judge you either way, what would you do?
- What would you tell your best friend in this situation?

Sit with what you know

What does your deepest wisdom tell you about the right path forward?

Letting the Decision Emerge

As you work through these questions, notice if a direction is becoming clear. Not with perfect certainty (that's rarely available), but with enough clarity to act.

For some partners, the answer is clearly to leave. The questions reveal that genuine change isn't happening, that safety can't be established, that what they need can't be found here. Leaving feels like the honest, self-respecting choice.

For some partners, the answer is clearly to stay. The questions reveal genuine recovery, growing safety, foundation worth building on. Staying feels like honoring something real and worth fighting for.

For some partners, the answer remains genuinely unclear. Some questions point one way, others another. The situation is in a gray zone that doesn't resolve neatly.

If you're in this unclear space, consider:

- Do you need more time? Is clarity still emerging?
- Is there a trial period that would help? ("I'll commit to six more months of working on this and reassess then.")
- Are there specific things that would tip you one way or the other? Can you articulate them?

- Would talking it through with your therapist or a trusted friend help?

There's no formula that produces the "right" answer. The decision emerges from your whole experience, your wisdom, your values, your gut.

Patrice's Decision

Patrice spent nearly a year living with the Five Questions. Her husband's recovery was real. She could see that. But something still wasn't settling.

"I kept thinking I should stay," she told me. "He's doing the work. He's changed. All the signs are good. But every time I imagined our future together, I just felt . . . heavy."

I encouraged Patrice to pay attention to that heaviness rather than arguing herself out of it.

As she explored it, she realized something: "I don't want to spend the rest of my life with someone I have to watch carefully. Even if he never acts out again, I'll always be a little bit vigilant. I'll always be wondering. And I don't want to live that way."

Patrice wasn't saying her husband couldn't recover. She was saying that even if he did, she wasn't sure she could fully trust again. The damage had been too deep.

"If I stayed, I'd be constantly managing my own anxiety, monitoring for signs, never fully relaxing. That's not a marriage, that's a surveillance job. I deserve better than that."

Patrice decided to leave. Not because recovery wasn't happening, but because the relationship couldn't become what she needed it to be, even in the best case scenario.

It was a hard decision. She grieved it for months. But she didn't regret it.

"I'm sad it ended. But I'm not sad I left. I left because I finally understood what I needed, and this wasn't it."

Brendan and Erica's Decision

Erica's journey went differently.

Her husband Brendan's recovery was rocky at first: inconsistent effort, defensiveness, what felt like grudging compliance. Erica had one foot out the door for months.

But over time, something shifted in Brendan. He hit a turning point in therapy when he began processing childhood trauma he'd never faced. The work deepened. His empathy grew. His engagement with transparency became genuine rather than resentful.

"I didn't trust it at first," Erica said. *"I'd been burned so many times. But I kept watching, and what I saw was . . . real. He wasn't just managing me anymore. He was actually changing."*

As Brendan's recovery became more genuine, Erica's sense of safety slowly grew. It wasn't fast. It took well over a year. But the trajectory was consistently positive.

"When I sat with the Five Questions, the answers were all . . . cautiously hopeful. Genuine change? Yes, I was seeing it. Safety?

Growing. Foundation? More than I'd realized. My gut? Scared, but also . . . something that felt like possibility."

Erica decided to stay, not out of fear or obligation but out of genuine sense that this relationship could become something worth having.

"I can't promise I'll never regret it. But I know I made this choice from a clear place. I wasn't staying because I was afraid to leave. I was staying because I'd seen enough to believe it was worth trying."

Honoring Your Decision

Whatever you decide deserves respect, especially from yourself.

If you decide to stay, you're not being foolish, naive, or weak. You're choosing to invest in something you believe has genuine potential. That takes courage.

If you decide to leave, you're not giving up, failing, or being unforgiving. You're honoring your needs and recognizing that some situations can't become what you need. That takes courage too.

If you're still uncertain, you're being honest about where you are. Continuing to live with the questions until clarity emerges is itself a valid choice.

Decisions Can Be Revisited

One more important thing: Your decision doesn't have to be final forever.

If you decide to stay, you're not committing to stay no matter what. If recovery stalls, if safety erodes, if you realize over time that this isn't working, you can make a different decision.

If you decide to leave, that doesn't mean you can never reconsider. Circumstances change. People change.

Decisions can be revisited when significant new information emerges.

This isn't about hedging your bets or refusing to commit. It's about recognizing that life is long, situations evolve, and wisdom includes knowing that what's right today might need reassessment tomorrow.

You're making the best decision you can with what you know now. That's all anyone can do.

The next chapters offer guidance for whichever path you choose: staying and rebuilding, or leaving and starting fresh.

10. If You Choose to Stay

The Path of Rebuilding

If you've decided to stay and work on rebuilding your relationship, you're embarking on a journey that will require sustained effort, patience, and courage from both of you.

This isn't the easier choice. In many ways, staying is harder than leaving. It asks you to rebuild trust with someone who shattered it, to become vulnerable again with someone who hurt you deeply, to invest in a future with someone whose past includes betrayal.

But for many partners, it's the right choice. The relationship has genuine potential. The recovery is real. The foundation is worth building on.

Let's talk about what rebuilding actually looks like.

Understanding What You're Choosing

Staying doesn't mean going back to how things were. The old relationship, the one built partly on deception, is gone. You're not reconstructing it; you're building something new.

This means:

Accepting that it will be hard. Rebuilding trust after betrayal is one of the most difficult things two people can do together. There will be setbacks, painful conversations, triggers, moments of doubt. Progress isn't linear.

Committing to continued honesty. The transparency you've established isn't a temporary phase. Ongoing openness is now a permanent feature of your relationship. It may evolve and relax over time, but the fundamental commitment to honesty doesn't end.

Allowing time. Rebuilding takes years, not months. Trust comes back slowly, if it comes back at all, and it can't be rushed. Expect this to be a long journey.

Continuing your own healing. Your recovery from betrayal trauma continues alongside his recovery from addiction. Both matter. You're not "fine now" just because you've decided to stay.

Remaining willing to reassess. Staying doesn't mean staying no matter what. If genuine recovery doesn't continue, if safety erodes, if you realize over time that this isn't working, you can revisit your decision.

What to Expect

Triggers will happen. Something will remind you of the betrayal (a date, a place, a phrase, a scene in a movie) and the pain will flood back. This doesn't mean you're not healing; it means healing isn't linear. The triggers typically become less frequent and less intense over time, but they may never completely disappear.

Some days will be harder than others. You might wake up questioning why you stayed, feeling the full weight of the betrayal as if it just happened. Then the next day, you might feel genuinely hopeful. This oscillation is normal.

Intimacy takes time. Physical and emotional closeness after betrayal is complicated. Chapter 13 addresses this more fully, but expect intimacy to be a gradual rebuilding, not an immediate return to normal.

His recovery will have ups and downs. Even genuine recovery isn't smooth. He may struggle, slip, have hard days. What matters is how he handles these moments: whether he's honest about them, whether he learns from them, whether the overall trajectory remains positive.

Protecting Yourself While Rebuilding

Choosing to stay doesn't mean abandoning your own needs and boundaries.

Continue your individual therapy. Your healing work isn't finished. You need ongoing support for processing trauma, managing triggers, and navigating the complexities of rebuilding.

Maintain your boundaries. The boundaries you've established don't disappear because you've chosen to stay. They're still essential. They create the structure within which trust can grow.

Stay connected to your support system. Keep the people in your life who understand what you're going through. You'll need them during the hard moments.

Keep paying attention. Choosing to stay doesn't mean turning off your awareness. Continue to observe how recovery is going. If you see concerning signs (recovery stalling, transparency slipping, old patterns returning), take them seriously.

Know that you can change your mind. If staying stops working, you're allowed to reconsider. You're not trapped by your decision.

What Rebuilding Looks Like

If things go well, over time you might notice:

Trust gradually returning. Not all at once, but slowly. You find yourself believing him more easily. You don't need to check as compulsively. Your nervous system relaxes more.

Emotional intimacy deepening. Conversations feel more real. You know each other better, not despite the crisis but partly because of the honest work you've done together.

Conflict becoming more manageable. You develop better ways of working through disagreements. There's more repair after ruptures.

The good days outnumbering the bad. The ratio shifts. More hope, less despair. More connection, less fear.

A sense of building something new. Not restoring what was, but creating something different: more honest, more intentional, more aware of its own fragility.

This doesn't happen on any particular timeline. It unfolds at its own pace, usually with setbacks along the way. The question isn't whether there are hard moments—there will be—but whether the overall trajectory is toward health and connection.

Supporting His Recovery Without Losing Yourself

You can be supportive of his recovery without becoming his manager, therapist, or caretaker.

Supporting looks like:

- Encouraging his continued engagement with therapy, meetings, sponsor
- Being willing to participate in couples therapy
- Acknowledging genuine effort and growth
- Giving him space to struggle without rescuing him
- Being honest about your needs and experiences

Losing yourself looks like:

- Making his recovery your primary focus at the expense of your own needs
- Monitoring and controlling his every move

- Taking responsibility for his sobriety
- Suppressing your feelings to avoid "triggering" him
- Putting your life on hold until he's “fixed"

Your well-being cannot depend on his recovery. If his recovery fails, you need to be okay. If his recovery succeeds, you need to have maintained your own sense of self throughout.

11. If You Choose to Leave

The Path of Moving On

If you've decided to leave, you're choosing to prioritize your well-being and future over a relationship that couldn't give you what you need.

This isn't the failure option. It's not giving up. It's recognizing that some situations, no matter how much work or love is applied, cannot become what you need them to be.

Leaving takes tremendous courage. You're facing the unknown, grieving a significant loss, and trusting that what lies ahead is better than what you're leaving behind.

Understanding What You're Choosing

You might be leaving because:

- Genuine recovery isn't happening
- Safety can't be established
- Your core needs can't be met here
- There isn't enough foundation to rebuild on
- Your deepest wisdom tells you this isn't right

All of these are valid reasons. You don't need to justify your decision to anyone.

The Fear of Leaving

Let me be honest about what leaving often feels like: terrifying.

You might be thinking: "What if I can't make it financially on my own? What if I'm making the biggest mistake of my life? What if he gets better after I leave and I missed out? What if I'm alone forever? What if I've wasted all these years?"

These fears are real and legitimate. And here's what's also true: people navigate these fears every day and build meaningful lives on the other side.

You don't need absolute certainty to leave. You don't need all the answers lined up. You need enough clarity to take the first step, and enough trust in yourself to figure out the rest as you go.

The Complexity of Leaving

Even when leaving is the right choice, it's not simple. You might experience:

Grief. You're losing something: the relationship, the dreams, the future you imagined. That loss deserves to be mourned, even when leaving is right.

Relief. Many partners describe a sense of a weight lifting when they finally make the decision. Relief doesn't mean the relationship was worthless; it means leaving was right for you.

Doubt. You might question yourself, especially on hard days. "Did I try hard enough? Did I leave too soon?" These doubts are normal; they don't mean you were wrong.

Guilt. You might feel guilty for leaving someone who has a disease, who may be genuinely trying. Guilt doesn't mean you're wrong. It means you have made a difficult decision that is right for you.

Fear. Starting over is frightening. Uncertainty about the future, financial concerns, worry about being alone: all of this is real.

All of these can coexist. You can feel relief and grief simultaneously. You can know you're making the right choice and still be scared.

Practical Considerations: Getting Started

Leaving involves real-world logistics that require attention. Here's where to begin:

Legal matters. If you're married, schedule a consultation with a family law attorney. You don't have to file for divorce immediately, but understanding your rights and options helps you make informed decisions. Many attorneys offer free initial consultations.

Financial matters. Make a list of: all accounts (joint and individual), monthly expenses, debts, assets. Open your own bank account if you don't have one. Get copies of tax returns, account statements, mortgage documents. Knowledge is power here.

Living arrangements. Can you afford your current home alone? Do you want to stay there? If not, where would you go? Can you stay temporarily with family or friends while you figure it out? Start researching costs and options.

Children. If you have children, consult with your attorney about custody arrangements. Document your involvement in their lives. Keep communication about the children separate from relationship conflict. (See Chapter 12 for more detailed guidance.)

Support. Write down the names of people you can call at 2 a.m., people who will help you move, people who will just sit with you. If your list is short, that's okay. Quality matters more than quantity. Consider joining a support group for partners going through separation.

These steps might feel overwhelming. Do them one at a time. You don't have to have everything figured out before you leave.

The First Weeks and Months

The early period after leaving is often the hardest. Here's what many partners experience:

The first 72 hours can feel surreal, a mixture of relief, panic, and "what have I done?" Let yourself feel all of it. Don't expect yourself to feel one clear emotion.

The first few weeks often bring intense grief. You might cry more than you expected. You might also find yourself sleeping better than you have in years. Both are normal.

Triggers will happen. A song, a smell, a familiar place: suddenly you're hit with a wave of grief or doubt. These waves get less intense over time, but early on, they can be overwhelming. Have your support people on speed dial.

He may try to pull you back. Promises, apologies, anger, pleading, you might experience all of it. Remember why you left. Write it down and read it when you're wavering. You made this decision during clarity; don't unmake it during a moment of loneliness or guilt.

The doubt will come. "Did I leave too soon? Should I have given him one more chance?" These questions are normal. They don't mean you were wrong. They mean you're human and this is hard.

Give yourself at least six months before making any decisions about going back. You need time to see who you are outside this relationship, time for the crisis fog to clear, time to trust your own judgment again

Taking Care of Yourself

As you navigate leaving:

Be gentle with yourself. This is hard. You're allowed to struggle.

Let yourself grieve. The loss is real. Don't try to skip past the grief.

Don't rush into anything new. Give yourself time to heal before making other major decisions or starting new relationships.

Continue your therapeutic work. You need support through this transition.

Imagine your future. Not just surviving, but thriving. What does a good life look like for you?

Rebuilding Your Life

Leaving creates space for something new, but that space can feel empty and frightening at first.

Rediscover who you are. You've been so focused on his addiction, his recovery, his needs. Who are you when you're not managing someone else's crisis? What do you actually enjoy? What matters to you?

Start small: What do you want for dinner tonight, without considering anyone else's preferences? What would you do with a free Saturday? What friendships have you neglected that you'd like to rebuild?

Create new routines. Your old routines were built around the relationship. Now you get to build new ones. Maybe it's a Saturday morning yoga class, or Sunday brunch with friends, or Thursday night pottery class. These new rhythms help create structure and meaning.

Be patient with the loneliness. There will be lonely moments: evenings when the house feels too quiet, holidays that highlight your aloneness, moments when you desperately wish you had a partner to share something with. Loneliness is painful, but it's not permanent. And it's different from the loneliness you felt in the relationship. At least this loneliness is honest.

Don't rush into another relationship. Give yourself time to heal, to figure out who you are now, to understand what you actually need in a partner. Many partners jump into new relationships quickly, only to discover they're repeating old patterns. Break the cycle. Be alone long enough to get comfortable with yourself.

Valerie's Leaving

Valerie decided to leave after watching her husband's recovery efforts for eight months.

"He was trying, sort of," she said. "But every time we made progress, something would slip. He'd miss meetings, get defensive, have some kind of slip he'd make excuses about. It was two steps forward, one and a half steps back. Endlessly."

Valerie she was waiting for something that wasn't coming: the moment when she could relax, when she could trust, when the vigilance could end.

"I finally understood: even if he eventually got there, I might spend years waiting. And I didn't want to spend my forties in this limbo of maybe-he's-changing, maybe-he's-not."

Leaving was painful. Valerie grieved the marriage, grieved the future she'd imagined, grieved the person she thought he was.

But she also felt something else.

"About a month after I moved out, I was walking my dog in the morning, and I realized I felt . . . light. Like a weight I'd been carrying for years was finally gone. I wasn't monitoring anyone. I wasn't wondering what he was doing. I was just walking my dog, and it was enough."

Valerie's leaving wasn't a fairy tale. It was hard, lonely at times, financially stressful. But she didn't regret it.

"I chose myself," she said. "For the first time in years, I chose myself. That's not something to regret."

You're Not Alone

Thousands of partners have walked this path before you. They survived the terror, navigated the logistics, endured the grief, and built lives they're proud of.

Some eventually found new relationships. Some chose to stay single. Some reconciled with their partners years later, from a place of genuine health. All of them would tell you: leaving was hard, but it was right.

You're not failing. You're choosing yourself. That's not selfish. It’s survival.

And whatever comes next, you'll handle it. You've already survived what you thought would destroy you. You're stronger than you know.

12. When There Are Children

Navigating This With Kids

If you have children, this entire journey becomes more complex. They add considerations to every decision, every process, every conversation. This chapter offers guidance for navigating the situation with your children's well-being in mind.

The Central Truth

Children need healthy parents more than they need parents who stay together.

This is important enough to repeat: What children need most is parents who are healthy, stable, and modeling good values, whether those parents are together or apart.

Staying in a profoundly dysfunctional relationship "for the children" often harms children more than a thoughtful separation would. Children absorb the emotional atmosphere of their home. They learn about relationships from watching yours.

This doesn't mean you should leave for the children's sake. That decision should be based on all the factors we've discussed. But it does mean you shouldn't stay solely because you think that's what children need.

Protecting Children During the Crisis

While you're navigating discovery, recovery processes, and decision-making:

Shield them from adult information. Children don't need to know the details of the addiction or betrayal. They don't need to witness your fights or hear you talking to friends about what happened.

One Exception: Safety Concerns

The general rule is to shield children from details. However, if the addiction involved behaviors that could directly affect the children's safety (such as exposing them to inappropriate content or people), you may need to share limited, age-appropriate information to help them protect themselves, ideally with guidance from a family therapist about how to do this.

Maintain stability where you can. Routines, predictability, and normalcy help children feel secure even when they sense something is wrong.

Watch for signs of distress. Changes in behavior, sleep, school performance, mood: children may show stress even if they don't verbalize it.

Reassure them. Without getting into details, let them know that whatever is happening between the adults, they are loved and safe.

Consider their developmental stage. A five-year-old and a fifteen-year-old have very different needs and capacities to understand.

What to Tell Children

Children often sense when something is wrong, even if they don't know what. Complete silence can be more confusing than age-appropriate honesty.

For young children: "Mommy and Daddy are going through some hard stuff right now. It's not your fault, and we both love you very much. Grown-ups sometimes have problems they need to work on."

For older children: "We're dealing with some serious issues in our marriage right now. We're getting help from professionals. We don't know yet exactly what's going to happen, but we both love you and will make sure you're okay."

For teenagers: They can handle more honesty, but still don't need graphic details. "Dad and I are going through some difficult issues in our marriage right now. We're getting professional help to work through them. I know this affects you too, and I'm sorry you have to deal with this uncertainty. We'll tell you more as we figure things out ourselves."

In all cases:

- Reassure them it's not their fault
- Emphasize that they're loved by both parents
- Don't put them in the middle or ask them to take sides
- Answer their questions honestly but without inappropriate detail

When Children Ask More Questions

Your children will likely ask follow-up questions: "But why? What happened? Whose fault is it?" You don't have to have perfect answers, and you don't have to explain everything.

It's okay to say: "That's a grown-up issue that I can't fully explain right now, but it's not your fault and both your parents love you." Or "Your dad and I are figuring that out with our therapist. What I can tell you is that we're both working hard to make things okay for you."

You're not lying or hiding; you're protecting them from adult burdens while still being honest about the fact that something difficult is happening.

If You Stay

If you decide to stay and rebuild:

Model healthy recovery. Children can see that people can make mistakes and work to repair them. This can be valuable learning, if the repair is genuine.

Maintain appropriate boundaries. Children shouldn't be included in your recovery work. Therapy sessions, Disclosure conversations, Impact Letters, these are for adults.

Get support for the children if needed. A family therapist can help children process the disruption they may have sensed.

Rebuild family connection. As recovery progresses and the relationship stabilizes, focus on rebuilding positive experiences as a family.

If You Leave

If you decide to leave:

Prioritize the children's stability. Minimize disruption where you can. If possible, keep them in the same school, maintain their activities, preserve important relationships.

Co-parent thoughtfully. Your relationship with your ex-doesn't have to be warm, but it does need to be functional. Children suffer when parents are in open conflict.

Don't badmouth their father. Whatever he did to you, he's still their dad. They need to have a relationship with him (unless safety concerns prevent it). Undermining that relationship hurts them.

Get them support. Individual therapy, age-appropriate books about divorce, reassurance from extended family. Children benefit from multiple sources of support.

Reassure them repeatedly. Children may need to hear many times that the divorce isn't their fault and that both parents still love them.

When Children Need Their Own Support

Watch for signs that your child may need professional help:

- Significant changes in eating or sleeping patterns
- Withdrawal from friends or activities they used to enjoy
- Declining school performance
- Acting-out behaviors or increased aggression
- Expressions of self-blame or excessive worry
- Regression to younger behaviors

If you notice these signs persisting for more than a few weeks, consider connecting them with a child therapist who specializes in family transitions. Early support can prevent longer-term struggles.

Nicole's Approach

Nicole had two children (ages eight and twelve) when she discovered her husband's addiction.

"My first instinct was to protect them completely," she said. "I didn't want them to know anything was wrong. But kids aren't stupid. They knew something was happening."

Nicole found a family therapist who helped her figure out age-appropriate ways to talk to her children.

"We told them that Mommy and Daddy were going through some hard things and were getting help to work on them. We emphasized that it wasn't their fault and that we both loved them. We didn't give them any details about why."

When Nicole eventually decided to leave, the conversation was harder. But she'd been building a foundation of honest, age-appropriate communication all along.

"The twelve-year-old wanted to know why. I told him that sometimes grown-ups have problems they can't fix, even when they try. That his dad and I tried hard but couldn't work things out.

Of course he wanted more. 'But what happened? What did Dad do?'

I told him, 'That's something between your dad and me that I can't fully explain. It's not your burden to carry. What I can tell you is that we both love you, this isn't your fault, and we're both going to make sure you're okay.'

It wasn't a perfect answer. He was frustrated. But I wasn't going to put him in the middle or make him choose sides. That was my job to manage, not his."

Nicole worked hard to maintain civil co-parenting with her ex. "I didn't do it for him, I did it for my kids. They need to love their dad without feeling like they're betraying me. That's my job to manage, not theirs."

Her children struggled at times, especially during the first year. But with support, stability, and reassurance from both parents, they gradually adjusted.

"They're okay," Nicole said, two years later. "Not unscarred; divorce is hard on kids. But okay. And they have two parents who are both healthier than we were when we were together. I think that matters more than staying together would have."

13. Rebuilding Intimacy

The Tender Territory of Closeness After Betrayal

If you've decided to stay, one of the most challenging aspects of rebuilding is intimacy, both emotional and physical. This chapter offers guidance for navigating this tender territory.

Why Intimacy Is So Complicated Now

Intimacy requires vulnerability, and vulnerability requires safety. After betrayal, safety has been shattered.

Physical intimacy may feel contaminated. The same body that touched you also touched others. The same person who was supposed to be exclusively yours was shared. He saw so many pictures of perfect women. Images, comparisons, intrusive thoughts may make physical closeness feel impossible.

Emotional intimacy may feel dangerous. You opened your heart to someone who hurt you profoundly. Being emotionally vulnerable again, letting him see you, know you, matter to you, might feel like inviting more pain.

Trust, the foundation of intimacy, has been destroyed. And unlike a building that can be quickly reconstructed, trust rebuilds painfully slowly, if at all.

There's No Timeline

Some partners find that physical intimacy helps them reconnect. Others can't tolerate it for months or even years. Some find emotional closeness returning before physical; others find the opposite.

There's no right way. Your process is your process.

Don't let anyone pressure you. Not him, not therapists, not cultural messages about what you "should" want. Your body and heart will tell you what's possible and when.

Physical Intimacy

If physical closeness feels impossible right now, honor that. You don't owe anyone physical intimacy, least of all someone who betrayed you.

If you want to explore reconnecting physically but struggle with it, here are some things that might help:

Go slowly. Start with non-sexual physical contact: holding hands, sitting close, brief hugs. Let your body gradually learn that his touch can be safe again.

Communicate constantly. Tell him what you need, what you can't handle, what helps. He should be asking, checking in, never assuming.

Expect triggers. Something might be fine one moment and unbearable the next. A position, a phrase, a time of day: anything might trigger intrusive thoughts or memories. When this happens, stop. Take care of yourself. Try again another time.

You can stop at any time. Even in the middle of things. Even if you initiated. Even if you were enjoying it a moment ago. Your body, your choice, always.

Consider working with a therapist who can guide you as you seek to establish sexual intimacy after betrayal. This is specialized territory, and professional guidance can help.

Intrusive Thoughts

Many partners struggle with intrusive thoughts during physical intimacy: images of their partner with others, comparisons, wondering what he did with them.

These thoughts are not your fault. They're trauma symptoms. Your brain is trying to protect you by reminding you of danger.

Some strategies that help:

Grounding techniques. Focus on sensory details in the present moment: what you see, hear, feel right now. This can help pull you out of intrusive thoughts.

Naming what's happening. "I'm having an intrusive thought. This is trauma. I'm safe right now." Sometimes naming reduces power. You can also let your partner know what is happening. He needs to be patient and caring when this happens, rather than annoyed or disappointed.

Taking a break. If the thoughts are overwhelming, stop. There's no shame in this. You can try again another time.

Therapeutic work. EMDR and other trauma-focused therapies can help reduce the intensity and frequency of intrusive thoughts over time.

Emotional Intimacy

Rebuilding emotional closeness is equally challenging. You're trying to let someone back into your heart after they broke it.

This happens gradually, through countless small moments of honesty, vulnerability, and repair. Through his showing up consistently. Through you risking a little bit and seeing how it goes.

Watch for genuine emotional presence. Is he actually there with you in conversations? Does he listen? Does he share his own inner world? Is there real connection or just coexistence?

Allow yourself to need him, cautiously. Part of intimacy is needing someone. After betrayal, you may have trained yourself to need nothing from him, to protect yourself through independence. Rebuilding intimacy means gradually allowing some need back in.

Notice what's growing. As recovery continues, is emotional closeness increasing? Do you feel more connected over time? Or does the distance remain–or even grow?

Charlotte's Intimacy Journey

Charlotte couldn't bear her husband's touch for months after discovery.

"Every time he reached for me, all I could think was: those hands touched her. That body was with her. I would literally recoil."

Charlotte didn't force herself. She told her husband she needed space, and he, in genuine recovery, respected that without complaint.

Slowly, over many months, things shifted.

"It started with just sitting next to each other on the couch. Then holding hands during a walk. Each little thing, I'd check: How does this feel? Can I tolerate this? And gradually, I could tolerate more."

The first time they were fully physically intimate again was almost a year after discovery. Charlotte cried afterward, not from pain but from a complicated mix of grief, relief, and something like hope.

"It wasn't like before. I don't think it ever will be. There's something lost that can't be recovered. But there's also something different. More intentional, more careful, more aware. In some ways, it's more intimate than before because we're both so conscious of what we're doing and why."

Charlotte still has hard moments. Triggers still happen. But the overall trajectory has been toward more connection, not less.

"I never thought I'd want him to touch me again. I was wrong. But it took a long time, and I'm glad I didn't rush it."

When Intimacy Doesn't Return

For some partners, physical and emotional intimacy never fully rebuild, even with genuine recovery, even with time, even with effort.

If you find yourself unable to be truly intimate with your partner despite wanting to, despite trying, this is important information.

It doesn't mean you've failed. Some wounds are too deep. Some trust, once broken, can't be fully restored.

You might feel tremendous shame about this. You might think, "He's doing everything right now. Why can't I just move past this?" Friends, therapists, even your partner might encourage you to "give it time" or "keep trying."

But you can't force intimacy. You can't willpower yourself into feeling safe enough to be vulnerable again. Your body and heart are giving you information, even if that information is painful to accept.

If intimacy can't return, you'll need to consider what that means for your relationship. Can you live with a marriage that lacks full intimacy? Is companionship and partnership enough? Or is intimacy essential to what you need?

Some couples do build satisfying lives as partners and co-parents without deep physical or emotional intimacy. They function well together, support each other, raise their children, but the romantic and sexual connection doesn't return.

For some people, that's acceptable. Intimacy wasn't necessarily their primary need from the relationship. For others, it's a deal-breaker. Neither response is wrong.

But living indefinitely in a state of "maybe someday it will come back" while knowing deep down that it won’t, that's a form of suffering that serves no one.

There's no right answer. But it's a question worth honestly facing.

14. A Final Word

Honoring Your Journey

You've walked a difficult path. From the shattering moment of discovery, through the painful work of understanding what you were facing, through Disclosure and Impact and Empathy and Transparency, through the quiet labor of living with the **Five Questions,** to wherever you stand now.

Whether you've decided to stay, decided to leave, or are still finding your way, you’ve done something courageous. You've faced a devastating situation honestly. You've sought clarity rather than hiding in denial. You've worked to make a decision based on reality rather than on fear, obligation, or false hope.

That takes tremendous strength. I hope you can see that in yourself.

What You've Gained

Whatever happens with your relationship, you've gained things that can't be taken away:

Self-knowledge. You know yourself better now: your values, your needs, your limits, your strength. The crisis forced you to ask questions you might never have asked, and the answers have clarified who you are.

Clearer judgment. After the disorienting experience of betrayal and gaslighting, you've learned to trust your perceptions again. You know how to pay attention, how to assess what you're seeing, how to listen to your gut.

Boundaries. You've learned to set them and hold them. You know now that your needs matter, that you have the right to protect yourself, that "no" is a complete sentence.

Resilience. You've survived something that many people never face. You've been to the bottom and started climbing back up. You know now that you can weather devastating storms and still be standing.

Wisdom. About relationships, about addiction, about recovery, about yourself. Hard-won wisdom that you'll carry with you into whatever comes next.

The Path Continues

The work doesn't end when you make your decision. Whether you're rebuilding or starting fresh, you're still on a healing journey.

If you're staying, the work of rebuilding continues: his recovery, your healing, the slow reconstruction of trust and intimacy. There will be good seasons and hard seasons. Keep doing the work. Keep paying attention. Keep taking care of yourself.

If you're leaving, the work of creating a new life continues: processing grief, building something fresh, rediscovering who you are outside this relationship. There will be hard days and liberating days. Keep moving forward. Keep believing in what's possible.

Either way, keep healing. The trauma you experienced doesn't disappear just because you've made a decision. Continued therapy, support, and self-care remain important. Be patient with yourself. You've been through something deeply significant, and healing takes time.

Some Final Thoughts

I want to leave you with a few things I hope you'll carry with you:

You didn't deserve this. Whatever happened, whatever choices you made before you knew, you didn't deserve to be betrayed and deceived. This wasn't your fault. It wasn't because you were inadequate, unattractive, insufficient. It was about his brokenness, not your worth.

Your decision deserves respect. Whatever you decided (to stay, to leave, to keep waiting), it's your decision, made from your experience, informed by your wisdom. You don't have to justify it to anyone. You don't have to convince others it was right. You know things about your situation that no one else can know.

The future is open. Whatever has happened, whatever you've decided, the future is not yet written. There is possibility ahead, for healing, for happiness, for a life that's authentically and fully yours. The pain you've experienced doesn't define what's possible. It's part of your story, but it's not the whole story.

You are not alone. Many others have walked this path. Many have found their way through to lives they love, lives with rebuilt marriages, lives as thriving single people, lives that don't look the way they imagined but are genuinely good. You can too.

Helen's Reflection

Two years after discovery, Helen looked back on her journey.

She had decided to stay. Her husband's recovery had proven genuine. They'd rebuilt something real, not perfect, not what she'd imagined, but real.

"I'm not the same person I was before all this," she said. "I'm sadder in some ways. I've lost an innocence I can never get back. But I'm also stronger. More honest with myself. Clearer about what I need and what I won't accept."

She paused.

"If someone told me two years ago that I'd be sitting here, genuinely glad I stayed, I wouldn't have believed them. I was sure I'd never trust him again. I was sure I'd never stop being angry. But here I am. Still married, still working on it, but . . . okay. More than okay sometimes."

Helen's path isn't everyone's. Other partners reach a very different place, thriving after divorce, grateful they had the courage to leave.

What they share, the ones who come through either choice well, is that they made their decision from a place of clarity rather than fear. They faced hard truths rather than hiding from them. They took care of themselves throughout. They trusted themselves enough to choose.

A Blessing for Your Journey

As you continue forward, whatever path you're on, I offer this:

May you trust yourself. May you honor your needs. May you find clarity when you need it and patience when clarity takes time. May you be gentle with yourself on the hard days. May you celebrate the good days when they come. May you be surrounded by people who support you without judgment. May you remember that you are worthy of love, of respect, of a life that fits who you truly are. May you find your way home to yourself.

Whatever path you take, may it lead you somewhere good.

I'm honored to have been a companion on part of your journey.

Should I Stay or Should I Go?

Deciding Your Future After Betrayal

Appendices and Reflective Tools

A Note Before You Begin

These tools are not assignments. They are not a test you can pass or fail, a process you must complete in order, or a measure of how seriously you are taking your healing. They are companions: resources here when you need them, organized around the five questions at the heart of this book, available at whatever pace and in whatever sequence feels right for right where you are.

Some of these tools you may use many times, returning to them as your clarity develops. Some you may find useful only once. Some may not feel relevant to you at all, and that's fine. You are the authority on what serves you and what doesn't. Trust that.

A few things worth knowing before you begin:

These tools are for your eyes only. Nothing here needs to be shared, not with your partner, not with your therapist, not with anyone unless you choose to. This is your private space for thinking, feeling, and finding your way.

There are no right answers. The prompts and questions in these appendices are invitations, not interrogations. If a question doesn't land for you right now, leave it. If it lands too hard, put it down and come back when you're ready.

The writing spaces are intentionally modest. These tools are not asking you to write essays. A few honest sentences, even a few honest words, are worth more than a page of what you think you should say.

Return as often as you need to. Your answers to these questions will change over time—because you will change over time. What feels impossible to answer today may feel clear in three months. What feels settled today may need revisiting after a new development. That is not an inconsistency. That is the honest, nonlinear reality of what you are navigating.

Finally: be patient with yourself. You are doing something genuinely difficult in the middle of one of the most disorienting experiences a person can go through. The fact that you are here, engaging with these tools, reaching for clarity, that matters. That takes courage, even when it doesn't feel like courage.

You deserve to find your way through this.

These tools are here to help.

Appendix A

Understanding Betrayal Trauma: A Self-Assessment

One of the most isolating aspects of what you are going through is the sense that what you are feeling is too extreme, too contradictory, or too irrational to be understood. That the intensity of your reactions means something is wrong with you, rather than that something genuinely devastating happened to you.

This self-assessment is not a clinical diagnostic tool. It is an invitation to recognize your own experience in a list of responses that are not extreme or irrational; they are the predictable, well-documented effects of betrayal trauma on the human mind and body. Reading through this list, many partners feel something they haven't felt since the discovery: the relief of being recognized.

In the weeks and months since your discovery, have you experienced any of the following?

Emotional Responses

- ☐ Emotional swings that feel disproportionate: rage, grief, numbness, and relief cycling through, sometimes within a single day

- ☐ Love and hatred for your partner coexisting in ways that feel impossible and exhausting

- ☐ Wanting desperately to believe him and being unable to trust anything he says, simultaneously

- [ ] A grief that feels like mourning a death, even though he is still physically present

- [ ] Humiliation, a shame that doesn't belong to you but that you are carrying anyway

- [ ] Guilt, even though you know intellectually that this is not your fault

- [ ] A terror of being alone that coexists with a terror of staying

- [ ] Moments of feeling completely fine—almost normal—followed by the ground dropping out again without warning

Physical and Cognitive Responses

- [ ] Difficulty concentrating or completing tasks that used to feel effortless

- [ ] Sleep disruption: inability to fall asleep, waking in the middle of the night, or sleeping more than usual as a form of escape

- [ ] Physical symptoms: nausea, exhaustion, a tightness in the chest, appetite changes

- [ ] Hypervigilance, a constant state of scanning for threat, checking, monitoring

- [ ] Intrusive thoughts or images that arrive without warning and are difficult to interrupt

- [ ] A strange flatness or numbness: periods when you simply cannot feel anything

- [ ] Memory and concentration difficulties: losing track of conversations, forgetting things you would normally retain

Relational and Identity Responses

- [ ] Difficulty trusting your own perceptions: second-guessing what you observe, what you feel, what you know
- [ ] A sense that the self you were before the discovery is no longer quite accessible
- [ ] Withdrawal from friends or family and difficulty explaining what you are going through or accepting support
- [ ] Difficulty being present in ordinary moments (at work, with your children, in conversations) because part of your mind is always elsewhere
- [ ] A questioning of your own judgment: how did I not know? What else have I missed?
- [ ] A loss of the easy, unconscious trust that used to make daily life feel safe

Reflection

Looking at what you checked, what do you notice? What has been the most difficult to bear?

Is there anything on this list that you have been judging yourself for, that you can now recognize as a normal response to an abnormal situation?

Everything you checked is a trauma response. Not a sign of weakness. Not evidence that you are too fragile or too emotional or handling this wrong. Evidence that you were genuinely hurt, and that your mind and body are doing what minds and bodies do when something genuinely harmful has happened.

You are not broken. You are injured. And injuries, with the right care and the right time, heal.

Appendix B

The Five Questions Journal

The five questions at the heart of this book are not questions you answer once and move on from. They are questions you live with, returning to them as circumstances change, as your clarity develops, and as the passage of time gives you the information that the questions require.

This journal is designed for exactly that kind of return. Use it as often as feels useful. Date your entries if you can; looking back at how your thinking has shifted over time is itself a form of self-trust rebuilding, evidence that you are learning to know what you know.

There are no right answers. There is only what is true for you, right now, with the information you currently have.

Question One: Is my partner demonstrating meaningful recovery?

This question is answered not by what he says but by what he does: consistently, over time, in ways that are visible and verifiable. It is a question about behavior, not about promises or intentions.

What concrete evidence of recovery have I seen in the past month? (Therapy attendance, recovery program engagement, honesty about struggles, changed behavior in the relationship, emotional presence)

What have I seen that concerns me, that looks more like performance than genuine change, or that feels like early recovery rather than sustained recovery?

If I set aside what he tells me and look only at what he shows me, what do I see?

Where am I with this question today, honestly? (Not where I hope to be, not where I fear I am—where I actually am.)

Question Two: Can I establish personal safety and boundaries within this relationship?

This question is about you and your ability to exist as a whole person within this relationship: to state what you need, to have those needs genuinely respected, and to maintain your own sense of self alongside the demands of the recovery process.

What do I need right now in order to feel even minimally safe in this relationship? (Honesty, transparency, emotional availability, space, consistency; be specific)

When I state what I need, what happens? Does he hear me? Does he respect it? Does he negotiate it away or redirect to his own needs?

Am I able to maintain any sense of my own life (my own friendships, interests, inner world) or has the relationship consumed me entirely?

Where am I with this question today, honestly?

Question Three: Are my core values and essential needs compatible with this relationship?

This question asks you to look at yourself, at what you genuinely need and value, and then look honestly at whether this relationship, at its best and most realistic, can provide that. It is a question about fit, not about fault.

What do I know I need from a partner and a relationship: not what seems reasonable to ask for, but what I actually need to feel loved, respected, and genuinely partnered?

What do I value most deeply, in a relationship, in a person, in how I want to live? What is non-negotiable for me?

Looking at this relationship honestly—before the discovery and now—how well does it align with what I need and value? Where does it fit? Where does it fall short?

Where am I with this question today, honestly?

Question Four: Is there enough of a foundation upon which to rebuild?

This question asks you to look at the relationship's history with clear eyes, not through the lens of grief, which romanticizes what you are losing, and not through the lens of rage, which can erase what was genuinely good. Both may honestly be present.

What was genuinely good in this relationship, before the discovery? What was real, what was warm, what was worth something?

What was difficult or absent in the relationship even before the addiction became known to me? What was I already living with—and living without?

After everything that has happened, is there enough goodwill, enough genuine care, enough basic respect remaining between us that rebuilding has something to work with?

Where am I with this question today, honestly?

Question Five: What does my deepest wisdom tell me about my path forward?

This is the question all the others are preparing you to answer. It is not a question of logic or analysis. It is a question of the deepest knowing: the part of you that has been paying attention all along, that is not fooled by performance or by wishful thinking, that has known things before you had words for them.

This question may not be answerable yet. That is completely

appropriate. But sitting with it—returning to it, listening for it—is part of how the answer eventually arrives.

When I get very quiet and set aside what everyone else thinks I should do, what do I sense about my path forward? Even faintly, even uncertainly?

What is the part of me that already knows saying? What is it afraid to say out loud?

What would I tell a close friend, in my position, if she asked me what I thought she should do? (We are often wiser about others than about ourselves.)

Where am I with this question today, honestly?

Appendix C

Meaningful Recovery Assessment

One of the most disorienting challenges of this process is trying to distinguish between genuine recovery and the performance of it. Between a partner who is actually changing and one who has learned what recovery is supposed to look like and is presenting that version of himself while the internal work remains incomplete.

This assessment is designed to help you see more clearly. It focuses not on what he says but on what he does: on behavioral evidence that is observable and consistent over time. No single item here is conclusive. Patterns, observed over months, are what tell the story.

Use this assessment periodically, perhaps every two to three months, and date your responses. The changes over time are as important as any single snapshot.

Part One: Recovery Engagement

Is he:

- ☐ Attending individual therapy consistently, with a therapist who has specific expertise in sexual addiction?
- ☐ Engaging genuinely in a 12-Step or equivalent recovery program: not just attending, but working the program?
- ☐ Maintaining a relationship with a sponsor or accountability partner who knows the full picture?

- [ ] Engaging with the deeper work: not just behavioral sobriety, but genuine exploration of what drove the addiction and why?
- [ ] Initiating his own recovery activities rather than requiring reminders or monitoring from me?

Part Two: Honesty and Transparency

Is he:

- [ ] Disclosing slips, urges, or struggles proactively without waiting to be asked or discovered?
- [ ] Honest about his inner experience of recovery: the difficulty, the temptations, the days when it is hard, rather than presenting a consistently smooth front?
- [ ] Following through on the transparency agreements we have established?
- [ ] Behaving consistently whether or not he believes I am watching?
- [ ] Honest about small things—not just the major ones—demonstrating that honesty is becoming habitual rather than strategic?

Part Three: Emotional Presence and Accountability

Is he:

- [ ] More emotionally present than he was during active addiction: genuinely available in conversations rather than partly elsewhere?

- [ ] Able to hear about my pain without becoming defensive, deflecting, or redirecting to his own feelings?
- [ ] Taking genuine responsibility for the impact of his actions, not just expressing remorse but demonstrating that he understands emotionally what he has done to me?
- [ ] Patient with my recovery process: not pressuring me to trust faster, forgive sooner, or move forward before I am ready?
- [ ] Showing up consistently over time rather than intensely in the immediate aftermath of a crisis?

Part Four: Warning Signs

Am I noticing:

- [ ] Promises that are not followed by corresponding action?
- [ ] Remorse that seems primarily about his own shame rather than about the impact on me?
- [ ] Resistance to transparency measures, framed as distrust or being controlled?
- [ ] Pressure, explicit or implicit, to move faster toward forgiveness or reconciliation than feels right to me?
- [ ] Behavior that is consistent only when the stakes feel high, and reverts when the immediate crisis pressure lifts?

Reflection

Looking at the full picture today, what does the pattern of his behavior tell me? Not what do I hope it means, not what I fear it means: what does it actually show me?

What has changed since the last time I used this assessment? What has stayed the same?

Date this entry: ____________________

Appendix D

My Core Values and Essential Needs Inventory

One of the quieter casualties of betrayal trauma is the gradual loss of contact with your own needs. When so much energy has gone toward managing his recovery, monitoring his behavior, and navigating the crisis, it becomes easy to lose track of what you actually need: not what seems reasonable to ask for, not what you can get by with, but what genuinely matters to you in a relationship and a life.

This inventory is an invitation to reconnect with that knowledge. It is not about him. It is entirely about you: about who you are, what you value, and what you require.

Take your time with this. Some of these questions may feel unfamiliar. If you have spent years organizing yourself around someone else's needs, being asked what you need can feel surprisingly difficult to answer. That difficulty is worth noticing.

Part One: My Core Values

What do I believe a relationship should fundamentally be?

What is a partnership for, in my deepest understanding?

What are the qualities I consider non-negotiable in a partner, not preferences, but genuine requirements without which a relationship cannot work for me?

What does honesty mean to me? What does it look like when it is genuinely present, and what does its absence cost me?

What are my deepest values about fidelity, spirituality, commitment, and about what we owe each other in a relationship?

Part Two: My Essential Needs

What do I need in order to feel emotionally safe in a relationship? What conditions need to be present for me to be able to be open, vulnerable, and genuinely myself?

What do I need from a partner in terms of presence and emotional availability? What does it feel like when that need is met—and what does it feel like when it isn't?

What do I need in terms of my own autonomy, my own life, my own sense of self within a relationship? What gets lost when I don't have that?

What do I need in order to feel genuinely loved: not just cared for, but truly seen and valued for who I am?

Part Three: Reflecting on the Relationship

Looking honestly at what I have written above, where has this relationship met these needs and values? Where has it consistently fallen short, even before the discovery?

Is there a version of this relationship—a realistic, evidence-based version, not a hoped-for one—that could genuinely meet the needs and honor the values I have named here?

What would I be settling for if I stayed? What would I be giving up if I left?

There are no right answers to these questions. There is only what is true for you. Keep this inventory. Return to it. Add to it as you learn more about yourself through this process.

Appendix E

The Foundation Assessment

Before you can decide whether a relationship is worth rebuilding, you need to look honestly at what existed before the discovery. Not through the lens of grief, which tends to romanticize what you are losing. Not through the lens of rage, which can flatten everything into a single verdict. But through both at once, with clear enough eyes to see what was genuinely good and what was genuinely difficult, honestly present and truly absent at the same time.

This assessment asks you to do that looking. It is not easy. It requires you to hold complexity rather than resolving it prematurely into a simple answer.

Part One: What Was Real and Good

Before the discovery, what did I value about this relationship? What was genuinely good, genuinely warm, genuinely sustaining?

What did I love about him: not the person I now know he was also being, but the person I experienced him to be in the good times?

What did we build together that had real meaning (a family, a home, a shared history, a friendship) that existed alongside the addiction and was not simply a fiction?

Part Two: What Was Always Difficult

Before the discovery, what was already hard? What needs were already going unmet? What did I already sense, even if I couldn't name it?

Was I already organizing myself around his needs at the expense of my own? Was I already making myself smaller, adjusting my expectations downward, accepting less than I needed?

What does the addiction explain about the relationship's difficulties—and what does it not explain? What might have been difficult even without it?

Part Three: What Remains

After everything that has happened, after the discovery, the disclosure, the crisis of early recovery, what still exists between us? What genuine care, respect, or connection remains?

Is there goodwill between us? Is there enough basic warmth and respect that the work of rebuilding has something to build on; or has so much been destroyed that what remains is primarily obligation, fear, or habit?

If recovery were complete, if he became, genuinely and sustainably, the person that genuine recovery would make him, would what remained be a relationship I would want? Would it be enough?

This last question is perhaps the most important one in this appendix. It asks you to separate the decision about the relationship from the decision about him: to ask not only whether he can change, but whether, if he does, what remains is actually what you want.

Sit with it. There is no rush.

Appendix F

Rebuilding Self-Trust: A Practice Guide

The betrayal has done something specific to your ability to trust yourself. The gaslighting, the deception, the experience of having your own perceptions systematically undermined by the person you trusted most, these leave a residue that makes it genuinely difficult to rely on your own judgment, your own instincts, your own sense of what is real.

Rebuilding that self-trust is not a quick process, and it is not done through positive thinking or affirmations. It is done through a series of small, repeated acts of honoring your own experience: of noticing what you actually feel rather than what you think you should feel, of trusting what you observe rather than deferring to his version of events, of acting on what you know rather than on what you hope.

The practices below are not exercises to complete. They are orientations, ways of being with yourself throughout this process that gradually rebuild the instrument the betrayal damaged.

Practice One: Name What You Actually Feel

One of the effects of sustained gaslighting is a disconnection from your own emotional experience. You have learned, over time, to question what you feel, to wonder whether your reactions are too much, too irrational, too sensitive. The first practice is simply to stop doing that. To name what you feel, to yourself, without immediately judging whether the feeling is appropriate or justified.

Right now, in this moment, what am I actually feeling? (Not what I think I should feel: what I actually feel.)

Practice this daily. It does not require writing. You can do it in the car, before you fall asleep, in the moment when a feeling surfaces. Simply name it. That's it. The naming is the practice.

Practice Two: Trust What You Observe

Your perceptions are reliable. The fact that they were undermined does not mean they were wrong. It means they were targeted. The gaslighting was evidence of how accurate you were, not of how mistaken.

When you observe something that concerns you (a shift in his behavior, an inconsistency in his account, a feeling in your body that something is off), practice trusting the observation before you negotiate yourself out of it. You do not have to act on every observation. You do not have to confront or accuse. You simply have to let yourself know what you noticed.

What have I observed recently that I initially talked myself out of? What did I notice before I decided I was imagining things?

Practice Three: Honor Your No's

One of the most direct routes to rebuilding self-trust is practicing saying no to the things that genuinely feel wrong, and meaning it. Not the elaborate, justified, apologetic no that anticipates his reaction. Just: no, this doesn't feel right for me right now.

This applies to the pace of rebuilding intimacy, to conversations you are not ready to have, to forgiveness that is being requested before it is genuinely available, to reassurance that would require you to perform a certainty you don't feel. Every time you honor your own no, you are building evidence that you can be trusted to know what you need.

Where in my life right now am I saying yes when I mean no?

What is one no I could honor this week?

Practice Four: Use Your Body as Information

Before the betrayal scrambled your perceptions, your body was telling you things. The tightness in your chest when something wasn't right. The ease in your body when something was genuinely safe. The physical sense of contraction or expansion in different situations and with different people.

Your body is still sending those signals. The practice is learning to receive them again: to check in with your body in the presence of your partner, in the presence of a situation, in the presence of a decision. What does your body say? What is the felt sense of this, underneath the story?

When I check in with my body right now, about my relationship, about where I am in this process, what do I notice? Tightness, openness, weight, ease? What is my body telling me?

Practice Five: Witness Your Own Progress

Self-trust rebuilds through accumulated evidence that your judgment can be relied on. One way to build that evidence is to track the moments when you trusted yourself and it turned out to be right: when you noticed something that proved to be accurate, when you held a boundary and it served you, when you waited rather than reacting and were glad you did.

A moment recently when I trusted myself and it served me:

Something I know now that I am learning to trust, even though the knowing came before the proof:

A Final Note on Self-Trust and This Decision

The fifth question—what does my deepest wisdom tell me about my path forward—requires that this self-trust be sufficiently rebuilt that your deepest wisdom can actually be heard. That is not a small thing. It takes time. It takes support. It takes the patient, repeated practice of honoring your own experience.

But it is available to you. The self you were before the betrayal, the one who trusted easily, who knew what she knew, who felt the ground beneath her feet, that self is not gone. She is recovering. And she is the one who will ultimately know the answer to the question this book is asking.

Trust the process of finding her again. She is worth finding.

Other Books by Dr. Chris Samuels

When you or someone you love is caught in the cycle of compulsive sexual behaviour, the confusion, pain, and shame can feel overwhelming.

For too long, sex addiction has been buried under stigma, misunderstanding, and shame.

In The 10 Things You Need to Know About Sex Addiction, Dr Chris Samuels brings thirty years of clinical experience to one clear mission: to help people understand, heal, and rebuild.

This self-care guide will support you in developing improved emotional awareness, increased stability, and better coping strategies to deal with the sometimes overwhelming emotions that follow the discovery of your partner's sex addiction.

By focusing on your personal needs and well-being, you will develop resilience in facing your relationship challenges and be able to establish a solid foundation for making informed decisions about your future, whether that involves reconciliation or a new path forward.

For more information about Dr. Chris Samuels' books, visit www.drchrissamuels.com/books

www.ingramcontent.com/pod-product-compliance
Lightning Source LLC
LaVergne TN
LVHW052314200926
848481LV00002B/559

* 9 7 9 8 9 9 3 2 8 1 5 2 0 *